Hockey's Greatest Moments

Hockey's Greatest Moments

CELEBRATING THE

BEST IN HOCKEY

Lance Hornby

KEY PORTER BOOKS

*To Margaret Hornby, who provided the
best memories of all.*

Library and Archives Canada Cataloguing in Publication

Hornby, Lance
    Hockey's greatest moments : celebrating the best in hockey / Lance
    Hornby.

Includes index.
ISBN 1-55263-632-1

1. Hockey. 2. National Hockey League. I. Title.

GV847.H67 2004   796.962   C2004-904808-2

The Canada Council | Le Conseil des Arts
for the Arts | du Canada

ONTARIO ARTS COUNCIL
CONSEIL DES ARTS DE L'ONTARIO

The publisher gratefully acknowledges the support of the Canada Council
for the Arts and the Ontario Arts Council for its publishing program. We
acknowledge the support of the Government of Ontario through the
Ontario Media Development Corporation's Ontario Book Initiative.

We acknowledge the financial support of the Government of Canada
through the Book Publishing Industry Development Program (BPIDP)
for our publishing activities.

Key Porter Books Limited
70 The Esplanade
Toronto, Ontario
Canada M5E 1R2

www.keyporter.com

Text design: Peter Maher
Electronic formatting: Jack Steiner

Printed and bound in Canada

04 05 06 07 08 5 4 3 2 1

I would like to extend my sincere appreciation to *The Toronto Sun* for giving me the opportunity to interview many of the people in this book over the past twenty years, and to work with such talented writers in the sports and news departments. *The Sun*'s news and library research staff—Julie Kirsh, Julie Hornby and Jillian Goddard—are also due praise for their tireless assistance. Michael Mouland, Anna Porter, Ruta Liormonas and Karen Moss of Key Porter Books continue to show great support.

Thanks also to Bob Duff, Canada's top hockey historian, who always fills in the blanks. Stan Fischler's *Rivalry* and Lawrence Martin's *Big Red Machine* were extremely helpful in unearthing quotes.

Contents

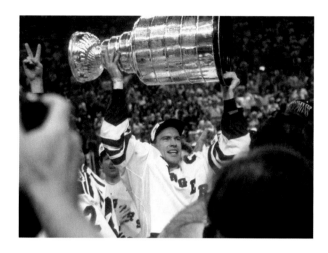

Souvenirs

Foreword

In my experience as a player, coach and broadcaster, I'm often reminded why hockey is such a great game.

To me, the mirror of our sport is the Stanley Cup playoffs. The owners stop paying salaries at the end of the regular season, so you see a lot of motivated players going hard for eight weeks, all chasing the magic that goes with winning the Cup.

Just when you think their bodies couldn't possibly give any more—such as in the great final in 2004 between the Tampa Bay Lightning and the Calgary Flames—they find something extra. It shows you the strength of the wolf is in the pack and tells me the Cup has not lost its lustre. Maybe the lure for these guys is not just the money.

We already know that hockey takes incredible athletic ability while balanced on a fraction of an inch of steel blade, but it's the personalties who have brought it to life.

There is a unique independence about the players, given that no other sport moves its kids out so young into the world to fend for themselves. It's become the same now for kids in Europe and the United States as it has been in Canada for many, many years.

Players develop an individuality I think is missing in other major pro sports. They're better prepared to deal with a lot of pressures, whether it's the game, the media or the travel. That's an asset, because hockey by its nature does not give a player or a coach a lot of time for thought.

> "There are so many former general managers and coaches in the NHL that we need two courses to play our alumni golf tournament."

In football, basketball and maybe even baseball, the game plan becomes more important than the player. But things usually happen too fast on the ice, sometimes violently. As a result, you get guys doing and saying things spontaneously. And unlike their counterparts, hockey coaches seem to be at odds with themselves, which provides a more revealing look at their character, as well.

That individuality is probably why hockey lends itself to so many great quotes and one-liners. When I was working in Vancouver years ago, we were losing at home and losing on the road and I told the press, "my failure as a coach is that I can't think of anywhere else to play."

A sense of humour comes in handy working on *Hockey Night in Canada,* but there's no shortage of memorable musings by others through the years for me to draw upon. Because you won't find people rooted closer to the ground than hockey people.

You hear it said that hockey doesn't have as many big, time stars to follow as other sports. That might be a weakness in selling the game these days, but then again, it's always been its strength.

Enjoy hockey and enjoy this book.

HARRY NEALE

Opening
Lines,
1890–1940

Let the Games Begin:
The Origin of The Stanley Cup

Since Lord Stanley, Canada's Governor General, put his thoughts on paper in March of 1892, his famous Cup has had the names of 116 amateur and professional championship hockey teams etched upon it.

Stanley never actually played the game, but his sons, Arthur and Algernon, formed the Rideau Rebels, and his daughter, Isobel, joined her brothers' games on the frozen ponds and rivers around Canada's capital. As a supporter of the local Ottawa league, Stanley came upon the idea of the Cup "considering the general interest which hockey matches now elicit."

As per Stanley's original instruction, a decorative bowl was purchased from a London silversmith for 10 guineas (about $50) and shipped from England to Canada. Its cumbersome official name — The Dominion Hockey Challenge Cup — was shortened to the Stanley Cup not long after the Montreal AAA team was declared the first winner in 1893.

The first Cup was just seven and a half inches tall and a foot across the top; it was, mounted on an ebony base

> **"I have for some time been thinking that it would be a good thing if there were a challenge cup which would be held from year to year by the leading hockey club in the Dominion."**
>
> – Lord Stanley of Preston,
> March 12, 1892

with a silver ring for the winning team's name. A second ring was added as more clubs joined the list, and more bands were jammed on until the entire trophy was ringed in silver. Team names were added to the decorative fluting on the bowl itself and when that, too, was covered, clubs started putting their names inside the Cup.

By 1924, players, coaches and management were being added to the winning team's entry, a practice that has been followed ever since. The Cup itself has not changed in shape since 1958, even though the original bowl was finally retired in 1969 to the Hall of Fame. In 2005, the current version of the Cup will be due for another facelift, as the five silver bands on the base of the trophy will have been filled up.

Unfortunately, Lord Stanley did not stay in Canada long enough to see his Cup be presented. In the middle of the 1893 season, as Montreal battled teams such as the Ottawa Generals for the Amateur Hockey Association title, he was recalled to England, where he passed away in 1908.

▌The Montreal Amateur Athletic Association won the inaugural Stanley Cup and repeated as champions the following year.

The Silver Rush: Dawson City and the Cup

In January of 2005, the folks in Dawson City will mark the centennial of a different kind of rush — their town's legendary attempt to win the Stanley Cup from the defending champions, the Ottawa Silver Seven.

The Cup was barely 10 years old in late 1904 and still a challenge trophy when its trustees were contacted by a colorful figure from the Canadian Northwest, Col. Joe Boyle. They accepted his offer to bring his team east.

Boyle was a Torontonian who had cashed in on the Yukon gold rush in the late 1890s and would later go to Russia to fight the Bolsheviks. He organized the "Nuggets" from a tryout of 20 players.

The unlikely assortment of men chosen for this wild 4,000-mile road trip included 19-year-old goaltender Albert Forrest. The rest were forwards: Norman Watt, Dr. Randy McLennan, Hector Smith, George Kennedy and defenseman Jimmy Johnstone, with Archie Martin as a spare.

Weldy Young, who played for Ottawa against the Montreal AAA in the first-ever Cup final in 1893, was both player and coach, but could not go because of his job commitment to the civil service.

The group departed Dawson City for Whitehorse before Christmas 1904, with some going by bicycle, while Martin, Kennedy and Smith traveled by dogsled. They took a train to Skagway, Alaska, but missed their boat to Seattle by two hours and had to wait five days for another. From Seattle, they backtracked to Vancouver for the train east. In Winnipeg, they picked up defenseman Dave Hannay, an addition the Silver Seven successfully protested.

Dawson had also wanted to add the great western Canadian star Fred "Cyclone" Taylor.

After 23 days of travel, the weary Nuggets arrived in Ottawa on January 11 with two days to rest before their two-game total-goal series. Predictably, they lost 9–2 in the opener, prompting Boyle to telegram Dawson and assure them Game 2 would be different. That turned into a 23–2 rout for the well-rested and well-oiled Silver Seven, whose one-eyed scoring ace, Frank McGee, notched a Cup-record 14 goals.

The Nuggets weren't discouraged, cashing in on their fame with a series of exhibitions in Canada and the U.S. on the way home. Their record was 11–13 in towns such as Trois-Rivières, Kingston, Brockville, Winnipeg, Brandon and Pittsburgh.

They arrived in Whitehorse on April 5. Watt, Kennedy, Johnstone, McLennan and Forrest chose to walk the last 400 miles from there to Dawson City, to a huge reception.

> **"The beating was not severe. We have a good chance to win the Stanley Cup."**
>
> – Col. Joe Boyle

In 1997, the Dawson City Nuggets Alumni re-enacted the journey to Ottawa to take on the Senators Alumni team. Ottawa won 18–0.

Humble Beginnings:
The First Night of NHL Action

Against the backdrop of World War I, and amid predictions of doom for professional shinny in Canada, the newly created National Hockey League played its first games, December 19, 1917.

The Montreal Wanderers hosted the Toronto Arenas, with the Montreal Canadiens visiting the Ottawa Senators. A fifth team from Quebec City pulled out just before the launch.

Despite the Wanderers' offer that all soldiers in uniform could attend the first game for free, only about 700 people braved the weather to watch a 10–9 win on an outdoor rink. The configuration of the surface had only one face-off dot, at centre.

It didn't take long for the Toronto media to set the ground rules for critical coverage of the locals as a *Toronto Telegram* four-paragraph report on the game showed. Under the headline "Poor Work in Goal Gave Game to the Wanderers," the eight local "Blue Shirts" were castigated for their play, especially starting goaltender Sammy Herbert and his replacement, Arthur Brooks, who came in for the second period.

One *Telegram* writer predicted that manager Charlie Querrie would be on the hunt for another goalie, another suggested that Querrie get Harry Holmes, formerly of the Pacific Coast Hockey Association, now living in Toronto.

Querrie laid down the law right away by posting six rules in the dressing room, including "First and foremost, do not forget that I am running this club" and "You will

> **"It does not require bravery to hit another man over the head with a stick. If you want to fight, go over to France."**
>
> – Toronto Arenas manager Charlie Querrie

not be fined for doing the best you can. You will be punished for indifferent work or carelessness."

Lt. Tom Melville was listed as the referee that first night, with Jack Marshall the "judge of play." A week before the game, the Wanderers feared they wouldn't have the required eight players. Sprague Cleghorn missed the whole season with a broken leg, and others were tied up in military service.

Ottawa had to start without the great Frank Nighbor, who could not get transferred from his Royal Canadian Air Force posting in Toronto until late in the season. On opening night, they were easy targets for the Canadiens, champions of the NHL's forerunner the National Hockey Association, in a 7–4 decision.

Under a headline, Victory for French, which had nothing to do with war in the trenches across the Atlantic, the *Telegram* reported Joe Malone's five road goals for the Canadiens, the NHL's first major single-game record, which would stand 51 years.

Assists weren't counted then, so Malone's 44 goals that season made him scoring champ. Ottawa goalie Clint Benedict fell down so much during that first game in making saves that the league scrapped the minor penalty for using such a tactic.

Later that season, a fire broke out in the Wanderers' clubhouse that burned down the Westmount Arena, throwing both the city's teams into the street.

The Toronto Arenas won the first Stanley Cup in the newly formed National Hockey League. They defeated the Vancouver Millionaires, champions of the Pacific Coast League.

THE ARENA HOCKEY CLUB OF TORONTO

   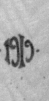  

1918   1919

CHAMPIONS OF THE WORLD

TORONTO ARENA'S
Stanley Cup Champions—1918

Top Row—left to right: R. CRAWFORD (Left Wing) H. MEEKING (Centre) K. RANDALL (Right Defence) C. DENNENAY (Centre)
H. CAMERON (Right Defence)

Middle Row: R. CARROLL (Coach) J. ADAMS (Right Wing) C. L. QUERRIE (Manager) A. SKINNER (Right Wing)
F. CARROLL (Trainer)

Bottom Row: H. MUMMERY (Left Defence) H. HOLMES (Goal) R. NOBLE (Centre)

This Phantom Scoring Ace Was No Ordinary Joe

For a player in a four-team league, Joe Malone certainly got around. From the formation of the NHL in 1917–18, through the 1920–21 season, Malone played for three different teams and led the league twice in goals. His biggest rush came in 1919–20, with the short-lived Quebec City Bulldogs, who spent only one year in the loop.

In 24 games, Malone accounted for 39 of the Bulldogs' 91 goals through the season's two 12-game halves. His most remarkable effort came on was January 31, 1920, when the Toronto Arenas were visiting and he racked up seven goals.

> "It was only a night's work as far as I was concerned. The only thing I remember is that it was very cold outside."
>
> – Joe Malone

Dubbed "The Phantom," he had a hat trick in a two-minute span of the third period, though freezing temperatures that evening kept the outdoor crowd to a minimum. No player since has been able to match or outperform Malone, not any of the golden-age players, and not even Wayne Gretzky or Mario Lemieux.

In the book *Rivalry*, Malone said it wasn't uncommon for a star of his caliber to play 55 minutes a night, with a couple of designated subs for forwards and defense. Goals were earned much more on individual play, as forward passing had not yet been fully adopted.

Malone had been born in Quebec City and played seven years for the Bulldogs when they were members of the National Hockey Association. Well-regarded for his on-ice demeanor in a rough-and-tumble era, Malone wound up with the Montreal Canadiens when the NHL was launched, as Quebec did not join the new loop right away. Malone had 44 goals and four assists in 20 games, using his trademark wrist shot to full advantage. After nine points in eight games in a shortened 1918–19 year, he had a career best 49 points with the Bulldogs the following season. Moving to the Hamilton Tigers for the next two years, he had a total of 52 goals before ending his career with Montreal as a bit player.

Seven NHLers have managed six goals in a game, including Malone in the same 1919–20 season. Newsy Lalonde had a half-dozen for the Canadiens three weeks before Malone's record, and brothers Corb and Cy Denneny did it for Toronto and Ottawa respectively in 1921.

Malone also had five road goals on the first night of the NHL schedule in 1917, as Montreal beat host Ottawa 7–4. That record was equaled several times, but stood for 51 years before Red Berenson of the St. Louis Blues notched six.

In a league that has become almost entirely defensive, the NHL could use another dose of Joe Malone. His 2.2 goals per game is a record that will surely stand the test of time.

Home of Champions:
The Montreal Forum

The Forum, which would become synonymous with the Montreal Canadiens, was actually built for an English Montreal team that no longer exists.

When the league was formed in 1917–18, the Canadiens and Montreal Wanderers both played out of Westmount Arena until a fire demolished the rink at mid-season. The Canadiens set up at the smaller Jubilee Rink, while the Wanderers folded, leaving the city's English speaking population without a team for a few years.

But in 1924, a group of businessmen raised funds for a 10,000-seat building that would run along Ste-Catherine Street. It was finished in just 159 days and was ready for its new tenant, the Montreal Maroons, who had entered the league with the Boston Bruins that year. The new building soon attracted the Canadiens as well, but the Maroons would raise the building's first Stanley Cup banner in 1926.

The Maroons would win the Cup twice, but the Canadiens soon established the more recognized stars, such as Howie Morenz, Aurel Joliat and Sylvio Mantha. By the 1937–38 season, the Maroons had fallen on hard times. They missed the playoffs and finally expired. The Forum was now the exclusive domain of the Habs.

> "The Forum brought us all together in our love for Les Canadiens and spawned heroes and heroic feats that will live far beyond the building."
>
> – Senator Hartland Molson

Though not as big or as technologically advanced as Maple Leaf Gardens, which opened in 1931, the Forum became the home of champions in the ensuing decades. Before the Canadiens would change addresses in the late 1990s, the Forum's rafters would be jammed with 22 Cup flags and the retired numbers of some of the game's greatest players.

The Forum was where Morenz lay in state, where Rocket Richard's glare burned brightest and where the fuse was lit for a city-wide riot in his name. Jacques Plante introduced the goalie mask there, the dashing Guy Lafleur brought fans to their seats and Patrick Roy talked to his goal posts.

Canada received its greatest hockey wake-up call at the Forum on September 2, 1972, when the Russians wiped the smug smile off the entire nation at the start of the Summit Series. Three years later, what many called the greatest game ever took place when the Canadiens and Red Army battled to a 3–3 tie.

The Forum experience was also about Roger Doucet's hearty "O Canada," Claude Mouton's bilingual P.A. work, Danny Gallivan and Dick Irvin in the broadcast booth, the organ, the fans, *chiens chauds* and many wonderful wintry nights.

The Forum was home to the Canadiens for a record 22 Stanley Cups, including a remarkable five in a row from 1955–56 to 1959–60.

Irish Eyes Were Smiling for the Leafs' Leprechaun

No one enjoyed the game more than Francis Michael (King) Clancy, a courtship that lasted seven decades.

He won the first of three Stanley Cups as a 20-year-old with the Ottawa Senators, hid the trophy, was acquired by the Maple Leafs mainly from the winnings of a horse race, played every position including goal, had a tribute night in which he wore a white beard and crown, was an All-Star defenseman, referee, coach and team executive, and ended his days as Harold Ballard's sidekick in the famous Gardens' bunker.

"King is the best thing that ever happened to the NHL," former Leaf Hap Day once said.

The glib Irishman was the center of attention everywhere he and the team went. His stories would often get so animated that pub owners would warn they'd stop serving him, only to find Clancy hadn't touched a drop of alcohol.

Clancy was one of the league's best defensemen in the late 1920s. An Ottawa native, he was given possession of the 1923 Cup for a couple of days to show it to his father, but when league officials went looking for the Cup the next year, it was missing. It was later located on Clancy's mantle.

The Senators of the day were cash-strapped. Leafs owner Conn Smythe came up with two players to deal for Clancy, but was short on the $35,000 needed to complete the trade. He laid a huge bet on a long-shot horse named Rare Jewel, and it paid off, allowing Clancy to become a Leaf in time for the opening Cup-winning season at the Gardens.

Clancy was paid well, which made him a curiosity for new fans and helped draw them in. He was such a boon to the box office that on St. Patrick's Day, 1934, the Leafs honored him during a game against the New York Rangers. He was pushed around the ice on a special float, wearing royal robes that revealed an all-green Leafs sweater. The Rangers protested after the first period that the jersey was a distraction and Clancy removed it.

After his playing days, Clancy became an official in 1937, at a time when the referees wore cardigans with shirts and ties. But he didn't stray far from the Gardens, where he was three times the coach of the Leafs. A relief stint for an exhausted Punch Imlach in 1966–67 is credited by many as inspiring the Leafs to their last championship. A pigeon pooped on his hat just before one of those stints behind the bench, and he refused to have it cleaned, thinking it was a lucky sign.

A few years later, his son Terry had a brief tenure on the Leafs. When King died in 1986, fans lined up right around the block of the Gardens to pay their respects, from Leaf greats and politicians to the kid who delivered his groceries.

> **"If I don't have fun, what's the use of playing?"**
>
> – King Clancy

First awarded in 1988, the King Clancy Memorial Award is presented to the player who best exemplifies leadership qualities on and off the ice and has made a noteworthy humanitarian contribution to his community.

A Black Eye for Old-time Hockey

Hockey did not get its bloody reputation by accident. The calls to curb its rogue element go all the way back to 1933, when Boston's Eddie Shore ended the career of Maple Leaf Ace Bailey.

Shore was already one of most feared players of his day, on and off the ice. On this particular December night at the Boston Garden, he'd been given a taste of his own medicine when Toronto defenseman King Clancy tripped him.

Livid that no penalty was called, Shore jumped to his feet and either mistook Bailey for Clancy or went after the first Leaf he saw. The reckless Shore rammed Bailey from behind, sending him through the air. Bailey landed, his bare head hitting the ice. Players on the ice recalled the awful sound.

Bailey's legs began to twitch as horrified onlookers summoned a doctor. As for Shore, he was rocked by a punch to the jaw from Toronto's Red Horner, who was enraged that Shore had not shown any remorse. Shore was cut on the head as he went down.

> **"I was never the type of man to hold grudges against anybody."**
> – Ace Bailey

A top neurosurgeon happened to be on duty at the Boston hospital that night, and after two operations to clear a blood clot, Bailey was allowed to return to Toronto. Bailey, who would never play again, briefly considered suing Shore, but was talked out of it.

The feud between the two men ended peacefully the next year. The Leafs organized a benefit game for their fallen teammate back at Maple Leaf Gardens, playing a collection of top NHLers on February 14, 1934. Shore was invited to participate. The Gardens crowd of almost 14,000 people went silent as Shore extended his hand to Bailey in the pre-game ceremony. But they burst into applause when Bailey accepted the apology.

The Leafs won the game 7–3 and a total of $29,909.40 was raised for Bailey, along with $7,800 collected at a Bruins–Montreal Maroons game. The special match became an annual event between the NHL and the previous year's Stanley Cup champion, and was the forerunner of today's All-Star game.

Players from both teams were interviewed by the Boston Police after the game. Had Bailey died as a result of his injuries, Shore would have been charged with manslaughter.

Morenz and Montreal: Made for Each Other

Before the NHL's Hart Trophy was 10 years old, Howie Morenz had won that MVP award three times.

Such was the impact of the Stratford Streak, who had 56 points in eight games as a midget player before the rest of Canada found out just what a great player he was. His fluid skating caught the eye of the Canadiens' management when his senior amateur team journeyed from southwestern Ontario to Montreal for a game in 1923.

From the moment of his first NHL goal on December 26 of that year to his retirement in 1937, Morenz would be one of the most exciting players in the game. His five-foot-nine frame and 165 pounds did not hinder him from leading the league in scoring in 1928 and 1931.

"He's the hardest player in the league to stop," Boston's grizzled defenseman Eddie Shore once said.

Where Morenz went, the crowds followed. He did what Wayne Gretzky would do 60 years later: sell the game to new American markets — in this case, Chicago, Boston and New York. When a new rink in Manhattan was being discussed, its financial backers would agree to it only if the league could guarantee that Morenz and the Canadiens would be there on opening night.

With Aurel Joliat joining the team around the same time as Morenz, the team won three Cups between 1924 and 1931.

But Morenz's career would end tragically. In 1935, when he first showed signs of aging, the Canadiens traded him to Chicago, and he drifted on to the Rangers. Unhappy to be away from the scene of his greatest triumphs, he was brought back to Montreal in 1936–37, only to break his leg in a game later that season.

Realizing he might never play effectively again, if at all, Morenz fell into a deep funk, which led to heart trouble and, eventually, death at age 36.

On March 11, 1937, his coffin lay at center ice in the Forum, as 50,000 people passed through, including the Canadiens, the rival Montreal Maroons and the visiting Maple Leafs. Some 15,000 people attended the service inside the Forum, and thousands more watched as the hearse made its way to the cemetery.

> "I thought there was nobody in the Forum. And I walked in I was aghast. It was jammed, but nobody was moving, this immense silence."
>
> – Montreal sportswriter Andy O'Brien

Regarded as the game's first superstar, Morenz won the Hart Trophy as league MVP three times during his career and in 1945, was one of the first to be inducted into the Hockey Hall of Fame.

No One Goes Home
Until Mel's Done

Mel "Sudden Death" Hill won two Stanley Cups, but his overtime heroics in a first-round series is what gave him his name.

Hailing from Glenboro, Manitoba, Hill was the least-known member of the Boston Bruins' top line in 1938–39. The trio featured center Bill Cowley (a future NHL scoring champ) and Roy Conacher of the famous Toronto-born hockey clan.

In the opening round of the 1939 playoffs, the last before World War II began draining the league's talent pool, the Bruins drew the New York Rangers. New York played a checking game to perfection, neutralizing Cowley and Conacher, who were both among the league's top 10 scorers that season.

The Rangers weren't as worried about Hill, a 10-goal scorer. Boston coach Art Ross took Cowley aside and told him to concentrate on getting the puck to the uncovered Hill. With 34 assists, Cowley was equally adept as a set-up man.

Game 1 between the clubs in New York dragged into triple overtime and was headed to a fourth period when Cowley found Hill for a 2–1 winner at 59:25 of extra time.

> **"We'd surround him in the dressing room after every one of his goals and say, "Is that all you can do? Why don't you backcheck more?"**
>
> – Milt Schmidt

Two nights later in Boston, the score was 2–2 going into overtime when the Cowley–Hill combination clicked again at 8:24. In 46 previous NHL overtime games, four men had scored overtime goals twice: Howie Morenz, Mush March, Paul Thompson and Frank Boucher. But none had done it in the same series in consecutive games.

And Hill wasn't finished.

The Bruins squandered their 2–0 lead in the series and a seventh game was required in Boston. By now, Hill had been dubbed "Sudden Death" by teammates and the media. He secured his place in playoff lore with another triple overtime goal, this one at the 48-minute mark, as Boston won the series with a 2–1 victory.

Hill had six goals in all during the playoffs that year, as Boston went on to defeat the Toronto Maple Leafs for the Cup. In the rest of his career, Hill had just six more playoff goals, giving him 12 in 43 games.

His only other brush with a big Cup goal was in the 1944–45 Cup final, when he opened the scoring for the Leafs in their 2–1 Game 7 win over Detroit.

Hill and his injury-riddled Boston team lost to the New York Rangers the following season, but found their way to the top again in 1940–41. Hill managed to score just one playoff goal that season.

Celebrating a Century of Patricks

The Patrick family might soon qualify for its own wing in the Hockey Hall of Fame, as they already go as far back as the Stanley Cup.

In 2001 Craig Patrick joined grandfather, Lester, father, Lynn and great uncle, Frank, in the Hall, as a member of the builders' wing. The Patricks have already had an NHL division named after them and a trophy in their honor for contributions to hockey in the United States, which Craig won in 2000.

The sons of a lumber baron, Lester and Frank were members of the Renfrew, Ontario, Millionaires, among the highest-paid players in the game at the turn of the twentieth century.

They went west to help launch the Pacific Coast Hockey League and inspired many of hockey's most significant rules and innovations before taking NHL management jobs — Frank with Boston, Lester with the New York Rangers.

Lester was 44 when he was pressed into service to play goal for the Rangers in a 1928 Cup final game. Starter Lorne Chabot had been knocked out by a shot to the head, and the Montreal Maroons would not permit any goalies in the crowd from taking his place. With a swig of whiskey for courage, Patrick stopped 17 of 18 shots for the victory en route to the Cup. Later, his sons Muzz and Lynn played on New York's 1940 championship club.

Turning a deaf ear to charges of nepotism, Lynn led the league with 32 goals in 1941–42. As he retired in 1946, sons Craig and Glen were entering the world. Lynn went on to manage the Boston Bruins, where the discarded goaltending equipment of stars such as Terry Sawchuk would find its way into his sons' ball hockey games. Feeling guilty after he grew up, Craig dug out Sawchuk's catcher and gave it to the Hall.

Craig played 401 games in the NHL, but made his mark as a GM, first as assistant GM with the 1980 Miracle on Ice American team, then with the Rangers and finally with the Pittsburgh Penguins. Making believers of a team that had never earned anyone's respect, he built Cup winners in 1991 and 1992 with a little help, of course, from Mario Lemieux.

"My dream when I was young was to be a player, then a coach, then a GM," Craig said. "I've lived my dream. I'm one of the fortunate people in the world."

> **"They wanted me to become a doctor or a dentist.
> But once the game's in your blood, it's in your blood."**
> – Craig Patrick

Although born in Canada, Lester Patrick made his mark on the game of hockey south of the border. As a result, the NHL presents the annual Lester Patrick Award to honor the recipient's contribution to the game in the United States. Grandson Craig was presented with the award in 2000.

War and Peace, 1940–1960

The Leafs' Comeback Cup of 1942

No one ever made a movie about the 1942 Maple Leafs, even though their harrowing comeback story of that year is better than most sports fiction.

The Leafs remain the only team in NHL history ever to be behind 3–0 in a best-of-seven Stanley Cup final and win. That the story unfolded in the middle of a world war that had been going badly made it all the more exciting for hockey fans in Canada.

> ## "What'cha worryin' about, boss?"
> – Sweeney Schriner

The Leafs were the favorites when they arrived in the final against the Detroit Red Wings, with home ice advantage to boot. But they fell victim to a clever game plan from Detroit coach Jack Adams. With the center red line not yet recognized for icing purposes, the Wings adopted a strategy of icing the puck and then out-skating and out-working the Leafs for goals.

It worked to perfection in the first two games at the Gardens, where the Wings earned 3–2 and 4–2 wins. In Detroit, they pumped five goals past Toronto netminder Turk Broda to put themselves in an easy position for the Cup.

But Leafs coach Hap Day was hardly a beaten man. He stirred up a hornet's nest for Game 4 by benching scoring stars Gordie Drillon and Bucko McDonald in favor of a rusty Don Metz and an unheralded Ernie Dickens.

He made a point of waving around Detroit newspaper clippings that predicted the Leafs' demise (even though most Toronto papers were saying it, too) and added a touch of schmaltz by reading a letter from a 14-year-old fan, Doris Klein, who implored her favorite team not to give up.

A Leafs director got in on the act by publicly condemning the Toronto players in hopes of making Detroit even more overconfident.

The Leafs fell behind early in Game 4, but won 4–3 as an irate Adams was suspended for the series for trying to go after referee Mel Harwood at the final horn. In Game 5, Don Metz fired a hat trick while on a line with brother Nick and Syl Apps in a 9–3 romp. Detroit collars started to tighten during Game 6, as Broda redeemed himself with a 3–0 shutout.

Game 7 drew the biggest crowd in Canadian hockey history at that time — 16,218. The Wings opened the scoring, but fiery Leafs owner Conn Smythe, who until then had not been able to attend the games because he was training his artillery unit, went into the dressing room to give the snipers a pep talk.

"We'll get ya a couple of goals," winger Sweeney Schriner promised. He did, indeed, score two, sandwiched around Pete Langelle's winner. No other club has yet matched the Leafs' rally in the final round, though the 1975 New York Islanders came back from 0–3 to beat the Pittsburgh Penguins in a quarter-final and came within a win of doing the same to the Philadelphia Flyers in the next round.

The Leafs thrilling come-from-behind win brought momentum to the organization. They went on to win five of the next nine Stanley Cups.

Meeker on the Mike

As a player, and later coach and broadcaster, Howie Meeker's had a love affair with hockey. But his career nearly ended with a bang during World War II.

He was one of the thousands of prime Canadian prospects who put their hockey dreams on hold to serve Canada in World Wars I and II. Many died or had their careers shortened or ended by injuries. Hockey Hall of Famers George Richardson and Scotty Davidson of the Toronto Arenas and American Hobey Baker all died in the 1914–1918 conflict. Scoring ace Red Tilson, who had led the Oshawa Generals to the 1943 Memorial Cup, was a casualty in World War II, as were Toronto-born Dudley (Red) Garrett of the New York Rangers and Leafs farmhand Jack Fox.

Meeker was almost was killed while training in England when a fellow soldier's grenade was thrown at his feet. "I would have killed the bastard, but they transferred him first," Meeker said.

The thousands of Canadians quartered in England before D-Day would often attend games played by powerful army, navy and air force teams at bases in Manchester, Brighton and Richmond. When a Nazi bomb tore the roof off the makeshift rink in Manchester, a tent was erected with a support pole sticking out of the blue line. "Better than a third defenseman," Meeker wryly observed.

He survived his grenade scars and landed in France a year later. Upon returning home to Canada, Meeker resumed his hockey career and was NHL rookie of the year in 1946–47.

On January 8 that season, the Chicago Blackhawks were visiting Toronto and were picked apart 10–4. Meeker skated off at the final bell content with what he thought was a hat trick. But earlier in the game, Meeker had casually mentioned on the bench that he thought he'd deflected a Wally Stanowski goal with his skate and that another Stanowski shot had possibly hit him in the posterior as it went in. Coach Hap Day overheard him and argued the case with the official scorer. When Meeker came off the ice, his wife was there to greet him with news of his five-goal game, an NHL rookie record.

After briefly coaching the Leafs in the 1950s, Meeker took a seat in the broadcast booth in 1968, mostly out of curiosity but also to act on his pet peeve that many analysts of the day either weren't critical or weren't students of the game.

Meeker dove right into the job, making no apologies for his behavior on the set or his high-pitched exclamations such as "Jiminy Crickets" and "Gee Whillikers." Meeker explained that using such trite phrases was better than swearing. "You're like an actor, you do things to disturb people," he said. "All I cared about was it would get people interested and talking about hockey."

> "I've got the worst voice in the world, I can't remember faces and names. . . and they want to make me a color analyst."
>
> – Howie Meeker

Although best known for his work in the broadcasting booth, Meeker was a very capable NHLer. He netted 27 goals in his rookie season with the Leafs, skating alongside Ted Kennedy and Vic Lynn on the "Tricky Trio" line.

The Haunting Tale of Bill Barilko

As Frank Mahovlich drove away from Maple Leaf Gardens in the spring of 1962 for a team function, someone shouted to him that Bill Barilko's body had been found.

The Big M recalls the shudder that went through him.

"Suddenly, everyone on the team made the connection between Bill's goal in 1951 and the fact we hadn't won until '62," he said. "I was stunned."

The search for Barilko's small plane had gone on for 11 years, but the mystery and mystique of the brash 24-year-old defenseman still remains today. A Stanley Cup–winning overtime hero, Barilko disappeared on a fishing trip that itself became the source of rampant speculation.

Wind the clock back to April 21, 1951. It's Game 5 of the Cup final against the Canadiens, and this game — like every match in this series — has gone into overtime, with Leafs up 3–1 in the best-of-seven. At 2:53 of extra time, the normally stay-at-home defenseman moved up, took a loose puck at the top of the face-off circle and fired it high at Habs netminder Gerry McNeil. The picture of Barilko flying through the air, the puck in the net and downed McNeil became famous.

"For our defenseman to be as deep as he was, at that point of the game [was dangerous]," teammate Howie Meeker said. "But that was Barilko.

"It was not a surprise. He was tough. When he did bodycheck, he really hurt people. It was like being hit with an end of a pickaxe."

> **"Bill Barilko disappeared that summer. . . the last goal he ever scored won the Leafs the Cup."**
> – The Tragically Hip, *Fifty-Mission Cap*

On August 25, a few weeks before the Leafs' 1951 training camp, Barilko and a dentist pal, Henry Hudson, took off from the Timmins, Ontario area in a single-engine Fairchild 24 pontoon plane. They planned a weekend fishing getaway and told family they would be home Sunday. They were seen starting the return journey, but disappeared on the way back from Rupert House, near James Bay.

A massive search was launched. Leafs owner Conn Smythe posted a $10,000 reward for Barilko, though many thought the disappearance was a publicity stunt. His equipment remained hanging in his stall at camp. As years passed, rumors surfaced that Barilko was alive and teaching hockey in Russia, where his parents had been born. He was also linked to tales of gold smuggling in the Timmins area.

In the spring of 1962, Ontario forestry helicopter pilot Garry Fields saw the sun reflecting off a piece of metal in heavy bush near Cochrane. Fields returned to mark the area and authorities eventually found the skeletons of Barilko and Hudson strapped to their seats, the plane nose-first in the ground.

Though witnesses say the plane appeared weighted down when it began its return journey, no fish remains were found in the pontoons, hence the smuggling rumors.

Barilko is remembered fondly in Toronto, where his No. 5 is retired, and the song *Fifty-Mission Cap*, which tells Barilko's story, remains a crowd favorite.

The Leafs did not win another Stanley Cup until the year Barilko's remains were discovered. They made up for lost time, winning three in a row.

50 Goals, 50 Games

Maurice Richard's pursuit of 50 goals in 1944–45 was followed with the same interest as the Allies progress across Western Europe, but nowhere more closely than in his home province of Quebec.

In Quebec, Richard was an icon, a flashy right winger with jet black hair and dark eyes that seemed to shoot sparks in the heat of competition. The Montreal-born Richard was dubbed "The Rocket" by local sportswriter Baz O'Meara in homage to his amazing speed, but his finish was soon the talk of the NHL.

After scoring five goals in 16 games as a rookie in 1942–43 (a season halted by a broken ankle), and becoming a member of the Stanley Cup–champion Canadiens in 1944, Richard began chasing the seemingly impossible 50-goals-in-50-games mark as spring beckoned in 1945. By that time, Richard was on the powerful "Punch Line" with center Elmer Lach and left winger Toe Blake.

"He was an arrow whizzing through the defense," a New York sportswriter said. "He did not know caution."

With 49 goals in 48 games, he came up empty against Chicago in an expectant Montreal Forum. That set the stage for March 18, the last day of the scheduled season at the Boston Garden. Harvey Bennett was the unlucky goaltender in the 4–2 Habs win, as Richard set his record.

On five more occasions, Richard would lead the NHL in goals, while Montreal would amass seven more Cups in his tenure, including five straight between 1956 and 1960.

It might have been six, but he was suspended by NHL president Clarence Campbell in 1955 for a stick incident with Boston's Hal Laycoe.

That skirmish triggered a riot in Montreal and left a significant faction of Quebec fans bitter at what they considered an anti-French conspiracy. In retirement, Richard conceded the French-speaking media was often harder on him than the English.

On October 19, 1957, Richard beat Glenn Hall of the Blackhawks to become the first player to reach 500 goals. Many of his regular season and playoff scoring marks lasted for years; his six overtime goals stood until 2004, when Joe Sakic caught up with him.

To recognize the Rocket's scoring exploits, the NHL created the Richard Trophy for the most goals in the regular season.

> "When [Richard] scored his 50 goals, he gave us all hope. French Canadians are no longer to be condemned to be hewers of wood and drawers of water, to be servants, employees. We, too, are the champions of the world."
>
> – author Roch Carrier

Despite the Rocket's remarkable 50 goals in 50 games, linemate Elmer Lach took home the 1945 Hart Trophy as league MVP.

Grounding the Rocket

How do you suspend a god? That's what an incensed population in Montreal wondered on St. Patrick's Day in 1955, as word spread that NHL president Clarence Campbell had ordered Maurice Richard to sit out the last three regular season games and the playoffs.

Richard had been in a scrap a few days before with Boston Bruin Hay Laycoe, a former Hab who used to be the Rocket's tennis partner. Laycoe high-sticked Richard during a rush, triggering the Rocket's much feared ballistic side. Twice he hit Laycoe with his stick, and as players and officials tried to intervene, Richard wiggled free from linesman Cliff Thompson and hit him, too.

At a hearing two days later, Campbell reminded Richard that he had not penalized him the year before in a similar incident in Toronto, but that a second offense couldn't be tolerated. Although he was leading the league in scoring and his team was in the hunt to recover the Stanley Cup from Detroit, Richard was declared through for the season.

"I was in the NHL office the afternoon the punishment was announced," *Toronto Sun* columnist Jim Hunt recalled. "The phone rang off the hook, most of the callers threatening [Campbell]."

> **"I know he had 50 goals in 50 games. And they named a riot after him. I think he had a temper."**
>
> – Teemu Selanne, on winning the Richard Trophy

The president refused advice from the Montreal police to stay away from the March 17 game against Detroit, as disgruntled Forum fans booed him and an ugly crowd of 10,000 gathered outside. A tomato was fired his way that splattered him and a female companion, then a tear gas bomb was set off, emptying the building at the end of the first period.

With Detroit ahead 4–1, the game was declared a forfeit and pandemonium broke out in the arena and the streets.

The crowd smashed windows all along Ste-Catherine St., and Richard himself had to make an appeal on the radio for calm before the mayhem finally ended. The incident cost Richard his only scoring title, and the fans weren't even happy that teammate Bernie Geoffrion had won in the Rocket's stead, booing him for the rest of the year.

The suspension fired up English–French tensions and, in the opinion of many Quebec intellectuals, was the impetus that launched an active separatist movement in the province over the next two decades. Richard would say later that he did not see the riot in such a broad context, but stuck by his guns that Campbell had made an error in judgment.

Despite losing their scoring ace, the Canadiens managed to make it to the Stanley Cup final, where they lost to the Detroit Red Wings. Richard, however, came back with a vengeance, leading his team to the next five Stanley Cups.

When I'm Sixty-nine: Gordie Howe Defies Father Time

By the time Mr. Hockey ended his career in 1980, he was a silver-haired 52-year-old playing with his two sons. But Gordie Howe still had enough jump for 41 points in 80 games and a plus nine with the Hartford Whalers, despite being much older than his coach, Harry Neale.

"How the heck do you tell a guy who's 52 about a team curfew?" said Neale about the unusual arrangement.

By 1979–80, the NHL had 21 teams that stretched to four corners of North America. When Howe started in 1946–47 with the Detroit Red Wings, there were six teams that traveled by rail and no televised games. The center red line was a fairly new concept.

Howe had learned his powerful skating stride on a slough that ran four miles along the edge of Saskatoon, while honing his playmaking skills on a neighbor's 80-by-30-foot backyard rink.

He'd tried out as a 15-year-old with the New York Rangers a few years earlier as the league suffered manpower shortages with so many players in the military. But Howe got homesick for Saskatchewan, and NHL history changed course.

The Wings came calling the next year and placed him in their Omaha, Nebraska, farm team. The big kid was summoned after 48 points in 51 games. "I remember thinking, 'Wouldn't it be great to get into one NHL game?'" Howe said.

> ## "It's pretty hard to forget old tricks."
> – Gordie Howe

In the next 25 years, Howe would play 1,687 games for Detroit, many as a member of the "Production Line" with Sid Abel and Ted Lindsay. The Wings won four Stanley Cups and made seven other trips to the final.

Howe followed Rocket Richard to the 500-goal plateau (leading Richard to candidly admit that Howe was a better all-round player than himself) and on December 1, 1960, became the first NHLer to reach 1,000 points. He left his mark on the record books with these and a few well-placed elbows.

Thought to be through with the game in 1971, Howe resurfaced in 1973 with the World Hockey Association, intrigued by the chance to play with sons Mark and Marty in a package deal engineered by his wife, Colleen. He had 100 points his first year in Houston.

The clan stayed together through a move to the New England Whalers and that club's entry into the NHL in 1979–80. He played in the NHL All-Star game that year with rookie Wayne Gretzky. Mark Howe would play almost 1,000 NHL games himself, ending his career in 1995 with the Wings.

At 69, Gordie would defy Father Time again during the 1997–98 season, playing a 47-second shift for the minor-league Detroit Vipers. The brief appearance, saluted by 20,182 fans in Auburn Hills, Michigan, made him the only man to play pro hockey in six decades.

❙ Mr. Hockey was also known as Mr. Elbows. Gordie's 801 goals were thanks, in part, to the fear he instilled in his opponents.

The Production Line:
Detroit's Big Wheels

Detroit qualified as Hockeytown long before a marketing whiz decided to incorporate the name in the late 1990s. Between 1949 and 1955, the Wings either finished first among the Original Six, won the Cup, or — on four occasions — did both.

The engine that drove these victories was the Production Line — Gordie Howe, Sid Abel and Ted Lindsay. General manager Jack Adams and his two coaches of the era, Tommy Ivan and Jimmy Skinner, often sought to break up the trio in an attempt to spread the wealth, but always came back to the Saskatchewan-born Howe and Abel and Terrible Ted, from Renfrew, Ontario.

> **"Gordie was the puck carrier, Teddy was the spirit and the drive. . . and I was more or less the garbage man."**
>
> – Sid Abel on the Production Line

The line almost stopped early in Howe's career during the 1950 semifinals. He lined up Toronto's Ted Kennedy for a hit, missed him and went head-first into the top of the boards. The gruesome injury required surgery to relieve pressure on his brain, a delicate operation that kept the radio station in Saskatoon on all night with updates for anxious listeners. Howe survived, but missed the first of what would be four Detroit Cups in the next six years.

The Wings weren't loved very much outside of Michigan. During 1954–55, Howe and Lindsay received cryptic warnings they would be shot at a game at Maple Leaf Gardens. And one night in Montreal, NHL president Clarence Campbell was sitting near the Wings bench, close enough to hear Vic Stasiuk swearing. The authoritative Campbell marched right up to Skinner and ordered him to exercise better control of his team. Steaming after a Habs goal seconds earlier, Skinner snapped and ordered Campbell back to his seat. When Adams called the next day, Skinner figured he would catch hell, but the boss only wanted thank him for standing up to Campbell.

"We used all that stuff to our advantage," Skinner said. "I'd tell the guys 'see, they don't want us to win.' [Montreal coach] Dick Irvin Sr. would tell the reporters there we had a bunch of half-assed players. That clipping would always find it's way to our dressing room board."

Yet the Wings didn't receive the kudos one would expect to follow such a great team. There were no post-game civic receptions and certainly no parades.

"If you were a Canadian player, your working papers usually expired at the end of the playoffs, so you had to get out of the States right away," laughed winger Johnny Wilson.

A local athletic club, not Adams, bought the Wings their Cup rings, and the players were expected back in the late summer for long goodwill bus trips to help sell tickets.

Howe, Lindsay and Abel combined for an amazing 1,369 goals and 1,804 assists in 3,447 career games.

Hockey Was His Life: Hector "Toe" Blake

His Cups runneth over. Hector "Toe" Blake carried Stanley twice as a left winger for the Montreal Canadiens, once with the Montreal Maroons and then eight times in his first 13 years as their coach.

"The Montreal Forum was his home," said one ex-Hab. "Even after he retired, he didn't have a lot of hobbies. Hockey was his life."

A superstar as both player and coach, he was an NHL All-Star left winger with Montreal, winning the 1938–39 scoring title and Hart Trophy, and a Lady Byng Trophy in 1945–46.

A native of Victoria Mines, Ontario, Blake played for the local Wolves team when it appeared in the 1931 Allan Cup. He began his NHL career with the Habs, a member of the Punch Line with Rocket Richard and Elmer Lach. In 1943–44, the line was instrumental in ending a 13-year Cup drought.

As a coach, he could be relentless, but he never pushed his team over the brink. He treated the greats, the marginal players, the French, the English all alike. But there were few slackers in the Canadiens of that era, as the Habs made the Cup finals the first five years he coached.

In the 1960s, a young man named Scotty Bowman was running the Montreal Junior Canadiens down the hall from Blake's office, and he lapped up every coaching tidbit Blake would offer. Blake's innovations included using the plus/minus statistic, and he was the first to give serious thought to line-matching.

"He had a good way about the way he communicated with the players," Bowman said. "He always seemed to say the right thing. If a player was having a tough time, he never tried to second-guess anybody."

Blake and Bowman sat on opposite benches on November 22, 1967, as Bowman cut his teeth with the expansion St. Louis Blues. He met Blake again in the 1968 Cup final, when Blake bowed out a winner with a four-game sweep of the Blues. Bowman would later make his name with the Habs, winning nine Cups as coach — one more than his idol.

"I don't think there is really that much comparison," Bowman insisted as he neared his own retirement. "The fact that I coached in the league 20-something years and he coached 13 years [means little]. They only had six teams when he was coaching. They only had two series. But they had the best players in the world on six teams. I don't know if anybody can ever equal [Blake's eight Cups in 13 years] or even get close to it."

Blake was a fixture at the Montreal tavern he operated in the years after he retired. He died in 1995 at age 82, after battling Alzheimer's disease.

> **"I didn't care what language they spoke, as long as they backchecked."**
>
> – Toe Blake

Along with his eight championships as coach of the Canadiens, Blake's name also appears on the Cup twice as a member of the Habs.

The Unmasked Marvel: Glenn Hall Brings Up Victory

Glenn Hall couldn't stomach success. He played a record 502 straight games by an NHL goaltender and was a cornerstone of the Chicago Blackhawks last Stanley Cup win in 1961, yet he rarely enjoyed the adulation due him.

Hall became just as well known as the goalie who had to gulp down a glass of water and throw up before a game to get ready for the fusillade of pucks he would face that night. He played most of his career without a mask.

"They used to think I was nuts," said Hall, who ranks sixth in NHL career wins, with 407, as we enter the 2004–05 season. "Then, most hockey people felt all goalies were a little strange. I needed that nervous stomach to play well. It improved my game and I'd do anything to improve my game."

The strange retching routine started in 1955–56, when his 12 shutouts for the Detroit Red Wings won him the Calder Trophy. Hall was so shaky that he threw up at the bench during a break.

A classic stand-up goalie, Hall's incredible string of consecutive games will likely never be broken in this age of 80-plus game schedules and strong backup netminders.

> **"Give me a place where I can walk into a field by myself and yell 'to hell with you' and hear the 'you, you, you' echo across the field."**
>
> – Glenn Hall

He was not replaced in a game for seven years, until a back injury took him out of Game 503.

He professed to hate the hockey life and was often a no-show at the Hawks' camp while he stayed home to "paint the barn." Yet Hall could never resist the lure of more money and somehow wound up back in the cage on opening night.

On a couple of occasions, the streak was almost halted by a puck to the head or a head-on collision in his crease.

"It's incredible," present-day Hawks goalie Jocelyn Thibault said. "I'm sure a lot of nights he was beat up."

Hall was credited with stopping the Montreal Canadiens' dynasty in its tracks in 1961 as it went for a record six straight Cups. He shut down Rocket Richard, Jean Beliveau, Boom Boom Geoffrion and Doug Harvey in the first round, completely blanking the Habs in Games 5 and 6.

Hall, who was a goaltending consultant for the Calgary Flames into his 70s, was modest about his accomplishments. "It's unfair to compare goaltenders from different eras because the game has changed so much," he said in 2004. Hall was a shoo-in for the Hall of Fame, with 84 shutouts and three Vezina Trophies.

Hall was left unprotected in the expansion draft after the 1966–67 season in favor of career minor-leaguer Denis DeJordy. The next season, Hall backstopped the expansion St. Louis Blues to the Stanley Cup final, earning the Conn Smythe Trophy as playoff MVP along the way.

Bill Mosienko:
Fastest Gun in the NHL

The following sharp-shooting tale could have taken place at the OK Corral, but actually happened on the ice at Madison Square Garden on March 23, 1952.

In the span of 21 seconds, Bill Mosienko of the Chicago Blackhawks fired three shots and three even-strength goals on New York Ranger goaltender Lorne Anderson. It's a record that still stands, with Jean Beliveau's 44-second power-play hat trick in a 1955 game against Boston coming closest.

Just a few days before his amazing feat, the Winnipeg-born Mosienko was thumbing through the NHL record book and remarked to a friend how nice it would be to have his name in it some day. The five-foot-eight right winger's chance came in the third period of a game in which the Hawks were trailing 6–2.

The first goal came at 6:09, with center Gus Bodnar controlling the puck from the face-off and finding Mosienko in stride behind Rangers' defenseman Hy Buller. Mosienko beat Anderson with a low wrist shot.

"It was my 29th goal, so I got the puck as a souvenir," Mosienko said later of his career high.

At 6:20, after Bodnar had won another draw, the play was successfully repeated, with Mosienko getting the puck past Buller at the blue line and going stick-side on Anderson. It should be noted that Buller was playing on a cracked ankle and the duo was taking full advantage of his lack of speed. The game was the Rangers' last that

> **"I don't think that record is ever going to be broken."**
> – Gus Bodnar

season, and the injury cost Buller a chance at a 36th point, which would have been a record by a New York defenseman.

With his milestone 30th goal, Mosienko once more fished the puck out of the net to keep.

The record-setter came at 6:30. This time, Bodnar directed the puck off the face-off to left winger George Gee. Mosienko came down the right side toward the Rangers' net, accepted Gee's pass, deked to Anderson's left and buried a high one over his left shoulder. Bodnar, who'd scored a goal early in the game assisted by Mosienko, also went into the books for the fastest three assists in a game.

"It was all a surprise as it happened," Bodnar said. "The way he was lining up, all I had to do was get him the puck. When [coach Ebbie] Goodfellow called us off after the third goal, I said I wasn't tired, because I hadn't even moved up yet. But Mosey was heated. He didn't want to go off."

A fourth Mosienko attempt on the ensuing face-off, again with Buller limping, just missed. "Bill, get off the ice, you're in a slump," Goodfellow said from the bench.

Just as important to the Hawks that game was that Syd Finney scored a pair later in the period to clinch the 7–6 comeback. Anderson never played another NHL game, while Mosienko went on to the Hall of Fame. He passed away in 1994.

Mosienko spent his entire NHL career with Chicago. A member of the "Pony Line," along with Doug and Max Bentley, he appeared in 711 games, netting 258 goals.

Glory Days, 1960–1980

Jean Beliveau:
One Class Act

How could two superstars co-exist on one of the most scrutinized teams in hockey history? The Montreal Canadiens had reason to wonder in the early 1950s, when the club installed Jean Beliveau into its lineup alongside firebrand Rocket Richard. But all the personal qualities that had served Beliveau so well as an amateur and minor leaguer in Quebec City would help him win over Richard and the rest of the dressing room.

Beliveau's grace under pressure was balanced by Richard's wild streak. When the Canadiens needed something to re-focus on after the end of the 1954–55 season was marred by the Richard Riot, Beliveau sprang to life with a league-high 47 goals and 88 points as Montreal launched a drive to five consecutive Stanley Cups.

Richard energized the team, but when he went off the rails, it was Beliveau, or Le Gros Bill as he was canonized, who could steady the ship. It's easy to see why all of Quebec City fought so hard to keep their junior and minor pro star, finding any combination of money and creature comforts to make him happy playing at home.

But on October 3, 1953, Canadiens general manager Frank Selke finally enticed Beliveau to sign, in a ceremony

> **"Each time when I left for [tryouts in] Montreal, the people in Quebec City would say 'Whatever they offer you, same here.'"**
>
> – Jean Beliveau

that was given front-page treatment. "We just opened the vault and said 'Jean, take what you think is right'," Selke said.

Beliveau would be part of 10 Cups in Montreal, accumulating 1,219 points in 1,125 games and a further 176 playoff points. He was a six-time first-team All-Star center, won the Hart Trophy twice, was the first ever recipient of the Conn Smythe Trophy as playoff MVP in 1965 and became the fourth NHL player to reach the 500-goal plateau.

He was team captain for 10 years, holding the honor until his retirement in 1971, when he led all playoff participants with 16 assists in a final Cup bow.

In all his ruthless run-ins with Canadiens through the years, Detroit's Gordie Howe said he would always shout "Look out, Big Jean!" before the hit so the respected Beliveau could protect himself.

In 2003, on the 50th anniversary of his contract, the Canadiens honored the 72-year-old Beliveau with a commemorative banner at the Bell Centre. It was also his 50th wedding anniversary, and his wife Elise and two granddaughters joined him on the ice.

NHL president Clarence Campbell said of Beliveau, "Any parent could use Jean Beliveau as a pattern or role model. He provides hockey with a magnificent image. I couldn't speak more highly of anyone who has ever been associated with our game than I do of Jean."

King of the Shutouts

Terry Sawchuk did not live long enough to enjoy this reign as the NHL's shutout king. In the spring of 1970, five weeks after his 103rd and final shutout, he died during some play wrestling at his home. Thirty-five years later, the retirement of Patrick Roy and aging of Ed Belfour ensures Sawchuk's shutout record will remain intact, at least until Martin Brodeur gets into his late 30s.

Sawchuk played 21 seasons and won three Stanley Cups with Detroit and one with Toronto. He was in goal the night the Leafs last won it in 1967. His name appears four times on the Vezina Trophy. A nervous man who had to provide for seven children, Sawchuk did not enjoy the trappings of life in the NHL and the pressure of his position.

He endured two severe injuries as a youth — a broken arm that went untreated for three years (he didn't want to tell his mother that he'd disobeyed her by playing football) and a skate blade mishap that almost cost him his sight in one eye. He survived a car accident while with the Wings that collapsed his lung, and he played much of the latter part of his career with a back condition that made sleep difficult.

> **"He was the best goalie I've ever seen. If you threw a handful of rice at him, he would stop every kernel."**
> – former Detroit coach Jimmy Skinner

Yet he was the best money goaltender of his era, according to peers such as Johnny Bower.

"I did the commentary for the [goaltenders'] book *Without Fear*, and Roy was ranked 1–2 ahead of Sawchuk by the authors," Bower said. "But I don't know if going 1–2 with Terry would have been wrong. Patrick seemed to be a step better over his career, but I'm prejudiced [to Sawchuk]. He did have 103 shutouts, which might never be broken now."

Roy retired in 2003 with 66 shutouts. Ed Belfour, 39, was closing in on 80 shutouts at the end of 2003–04.

"One hundred and three, that's unbelievable, incredible," Belfour said. "No one's going to catch Terry."

When reminded that players in the 1950s and most of the 1960s did not have curved sticks that Belfour now faces, Belfour pointed out that Sawchuk played most of his career without a mask.

Sawchuk should have retired a Red Wing, but he was traded to Boston when Detroit tried to make room for Glenn Hall. After he and Bower helped the Leafs to the 1967 Cup, he became the first man chosen in the historic expansion draft, going to the Los Angeles Kings before finally ending his career with the New York Rangers.

A star from the beginning, Sawchuk took home the Calder Trophy as rookie of the year in 1951. He won the Vezina Trophy for best goaltender the next two seasons and added two others during his illustrious career.

The Man Behind the Mask

Even in the weird world of goaltenders, Jacques Plante followed a different drummer. He roamed from his cage, he handled the puck, he was the first to wear a mask as a habit, he knit his own toques. He was Quebec-born and a Habs star, yet he played for three of the Canadiens' Original Six rivals (the Leafs, the Bruins and the Rangers), as well as a stint in the WHA.

In his later years, the eccentric stopper refused to stay with the team on certain floors of certain hotels because they were bad for his breathing.

But there is no denying Jake the Snake's imprint on the game: seven Vezina Trophies, as well as the evolution of face protection for those in hockey's most dangerous position.

Plante's arrival in the NHL was a dramatic one, in the midst of the 1953 playoffs with Montreal down 3–2 in a series with the Chicago Blackhawks. Bumping Gerry McNeil from the cage, Plante won that first start 3–0 and then Game 7 by a 3–1 score. He also staked the Habs to a 2–0 series lead against Boston in the final, before coach Dick Irvin brought McNeil back and the team went on to the Cup. McNeil was gone after the next year, and Plante became number one on a team about to win five consecutive Cups.

> **"When I was a youngster, all I ever wanted to do was play one game for the big team, the Montreal Canadiens."**
>
> – Jacques Plante

In those days, taking a puck in the head was almost considered a badge of honor for a goaltender. The idea of a backup had yet to be embraced, so the victim was cleaned up, stitched up and sent back in. Plante changed that school of thought on November 1, 1959.

Andy Bathgate of the Rangers fired a puck into Plante's face, admitting years later that he'd purposely shot high to avenge a tripping infraction by the Habs. Plante reportly took 20 stitches. He had already received 400 stitches in the course of his career. He had also had his nose broken four times, his skull fractured twice and a cheekbone broken twice.

Plante thought it was the perfect time to get out the mask he'd been experimenting with, even though coach Hector "Toe" Blake dismissed the crude contraption as a sign his man had lost his nerve. Clint Benedict and Charlie Raynor had used one sparingly years before, but this innovation became a part of Plante's standard equipment.

Soon, all goalies had adopted some form of the mask. In addition to its safety benefits, mask design has become an art form in the game. Plante played until he was 44. He passed away in 1986.

Plante won seven Vezina Trophies during his 19 year NHL career, the last of which came in 1969, the year he came back after four years of retirement.

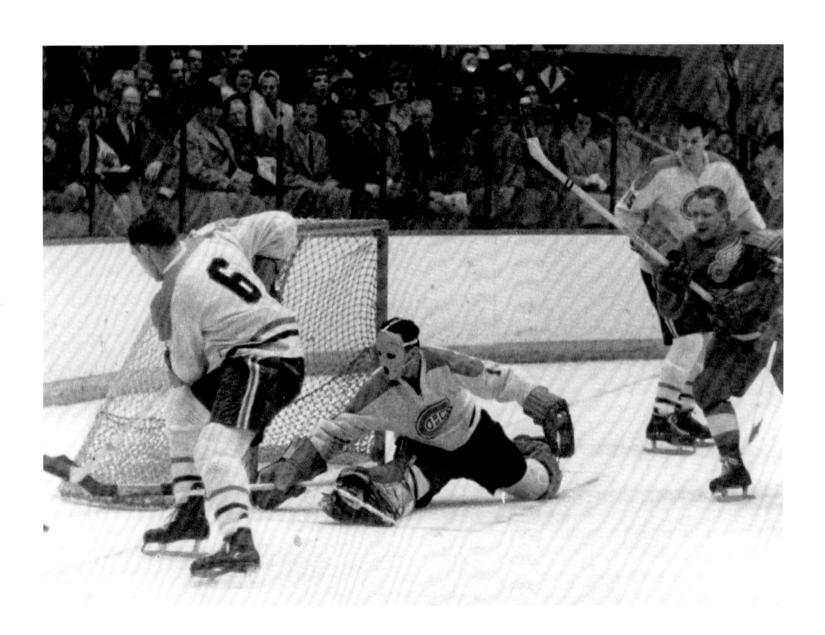

A Hero Without a Leg to Stand On

By all rights, Bob Baun's career should have ended in the 1964 Stanley Cup final. Instead, the series spawned the greatest injury comeback story in Maple Leaf and NHL playoff history.

Tell any player oozing from a high sticking or with a shoulder dangling from a socket to take himself out of a post-season game, and he'll undoubtedly argue that if Boomer Baun could score an overtime goal on a broken leg, then he had to stay in.

It was April 23, 1964, and the host Detroit Red Wings were leading the Leafs 3–2 and looking to stop Toronto's bid for a third consecutive Cup. About seven minutes into the third, Gordie Howe put some mustard on a hard dump-in pass that caught Baun's right leg below the shin guard and above the skate boot.

Baun labored on for a few minutes until his busted pin could not support him and he went down. A stretcher was called, and he left the game, collapsing near goaltender Johnny Bower. Regulation time expired with the score 3–3.

As the Leafs huddled in the Olympia dressing room, Baun asked club doctor Jim Murray to tape or freeze the leg so he could continue. Baun went over coach Punch Imlach's head and told defenseman Kent Douglas to stay on the bench so he could return.

> **"I heard a boom like a cannon. It was the bone cracking."**
>
> – Bob Baun

In overtime, Baun intercepted a Wings' breakout pass along the boards and fired it back. With a fortuitous bounce off of Bill Gadsby's stick (Baun playfully called him Jinxie the rest of their careers) the puck wound up in the net.

"I forgot all about the pain," Baun said. "It was a knuckleball. I watched it all the way in."

Baun refused requests to have the leg X-rayed before Game 7 and hid at a friend's farm to avoid club medical personnel. The Leafs went on to win Game 7 by a 4–0 count, with Baun in pain, but still in the lineup.

As he limped around a victory party at Leaf exec Stafford Smythe's home, he was urged to have the leg X-rayed. When he finally went to the hospital, an x-ray showed a cracked bone above the ankle. Earlier in his career, he had survived a 143-stitch cut on his head and had his throat nearly slashed by a skate.

"I guess it was my pain tolerance and the mental ability to block out things," Baun said.

Baun, who won four Cups with Toronto, had 3 playoff goals in 96 career playoff games. Two of them came in that 1964 series. Gadsby played 67 games and never won a Cup.

An unlikely hero, Baun managed to score just 40 NHL goals in 1,060 career regular season and playoff games.

The Adjuster

The success and satisfaction Carl Brewer sought in the game of hockey came two decades after his playing days were through.

Brewer will certainly be regarded as one of the finest defensemen in the history of the Maple Leafs, with his name on three straight Stanley Cups between 1962 and 1964. He was also an NHL second-team All-Star in 1962.

"He was the forerunner of Bobby Orr," teammate Bob Baun said. "His [mind] and body moved together."

But the restless Brewer, who at one time considered the priesthood or a teaching vocation, wanted more from the hockey experience. He walked out on the Leafs and overbearing coach Punch Imlach in 1965, getting his degree in French and political science.

Brewer's journey of discovery took him back to the game's roots, with a tryout for Canada's national team, composed of many university-educated kids under the tutelage of Father David Bauer. A free-wheeling defenseman, Brewer delighted playing on the wide European surfaces during a stop as player/coach in Finland. He was one of the first North Americans to get a peek at what the Russians were up to in their hockey labs before the 1972 Summit Series.

> **"Present-day players should look back and put up a plaque for Carl Brewer. He's the one who put a lot of money in their pockets."**
> – Gordie Howe

In all, Brewer retired from hockey five times, making one last improbable comeback in 1980 at age 41 with the Leafs, under GM Imlach, no less.

But it was a pay dispute that year with the Leafs over his 20-game stint that suddenly drew his interest Players' Union boss Alan Eagleson. A one-time client of Eagleson's, Brewer became suspicious of where union pension money had been funneled and he was concerned about Eagelson's cozy relationship with NHL president John Ziegler.

Brewer had finally found his raison d'être, researching and launching a $45-million suit on behalf of 1,300 league pensioners in the 1990s. He gathered Gordie Howe and some of the biggest names from the league's alumni to give the cause some star power and win over an initially doubtful public.

The league eventually had to pay the money, but Eagleson's role was still a subject of controversy. The joint efforts of Brewer, American author Russ Conway and law enforcement agencies on both sides of the border led to Eagleson serving jail time in Canada.

Former defenseman Brad Park perhaps said it best when he noted, "Carl sacrificed a lot for the good of hockey."

A warrior on and off the ice, Brewer retired from the St. Louis Blues in 1972 and then resurfaced with the Maple Leafs in 1979 at the age of 41.

The Leafs Steal the Summer of Love

Since 1967, the center of the hockey universe has had a black hole. For all the attention the game gets in Hogtown, the Maple Leafs and their die-hard fans enter the 2004–05 season still saluting the last Toronto Stanley Cup champions, during Canada's centennial. With every gray hair the '67 Leafs add, the silver on their Cup shines brighter.

"We never thought that we'd be the last team to win it," defenseman Allan Stanley said. "When they let me go for a youth movement [in 1968], I often joked, 'They'll never win another Cup without me'. But geez, I didn't mean it."

The Summer of Love beckoned in 1967 as the underdog Leafs entered the playoffs with an average age of 31.2.

"That year will always stand out because of we older players," goaltender Johnny Bower said. "There was a definite feeling that some of us wouldn't get another chance."

The up-and-down season had already seen a club record 10-game losing streak, and coach Punch Imlach checked into hospital for exhaustion. The underdog Leafs arrived in the opening round to face the top-ranked Chicago Blackhawks.

Chicago boasted Bobby Hull and Stan Mikita. But Bower and Terry Sawchuk were magnificent in goal. Sawchuk, aching from head to toe with injuries, earned the most kudos during the six-game series victory.

> **"They may not have been the best players, but they never quit, never let me beat them and they sure as hell weren't going to let the other team win."**
>
> – Punch Imlach

"That series was the bigger upset," defenseman Marcel Pronovost contends. "But everyone remembers Montreal in the next round."

Montreal was also favored, but Imlach prepared his team well with a checking plan to keep the faster Habs to the outside, compensating for Toronto's plodding skaters. Four primary defensemen figured in the scheme, along with a two-way line of Bob Pulford, Jim Pappin and Peter Stemkowski.

Imlach was at his showman/superstitious best, getting under the skin of rival Toe Blake. He told Montreal writers that a "Junior B goalie" (Rogie Vachon) would not beat his team. He had the Leafs watch films of Toronto's three straight Cups between 1962 and 1964.

After a Game 4 loss, Imlach cut out the pictures of the celebrating Habs and put them around the dressing room. Before the Game 6 clincher, he dumped a pile of money in the middle of the room, barked, "This is what it's all about" and walked out.

With the score 2–1 and Montreal goalie Gump Worsley on the bench, Imlach called on most of his older players — George Armstrong, Red Kelly, Tom Horton, Allan Stanley and Bob Pulford — for a last-minute face-off near Sawchuk. Stanley was instructed to move up and take the draw to tie up Jean Beliveau, which he did to perfection, leading to Armstrong's empty-net goal.

The Leafs have not advanced to the finals since their victory in 1967. Their fans have been forced to endure many close calls, most recently, a six-game loss to the Carolina Hurricanes in the 2002 Eastern Conference final.

Excitement Was Orr's Calling Card

In 1966, a player of Bobby Orr's offensive creativity was bound to make a big impact. The man who would redefine the position of defenseman arrived from the Oshawa Generals' juniors to lead the downtrodden Boston Bruins to the promised land.

"Those four years I spent playing in Oshawa were four of the best years of my life," Orr said. "I liked to skate and take the puck and go. That wasn't the way a defenseman was supposed to play. The Bruins never tried to change me."

He won eight straight Norris Trophies as top defenseman, but more significantly, led the league in scoring twice. In a memorable stretch between 1969–70 and 1974–75, Orr had six consecutive 100-plus point seasons.

In New England, the two Stanley Cup teams that Orr inspired were responsible for a hockey boom that resonates into the 21st century. The region will certainly never forget the afternoon when 29 years of Cup futility came to an end. The B's faced the St. Louis Blues with a chance to sweep at home.

Up to then, Blues coach Scotty Bowman had been successful in shadowing Orr in the final by using another defenseman, Jim Roberts. But Orr's only goal in the series would be one for the ages, coming at 40 seconds of overtime.

He was tripped up in the crease as he moved in on a gamble and knocked in a Derek Sanderson pass. Orr was caught in a famous still photograph as he soared through the air.

"A spectacular goal by a spectacular player," Boston coach Harry Sinden said.

There would be a second Cup for the Bruins in 1972, with Orr getting 19 assists through the post-season, including eight against the New York Rangers in the final. He had the Cup-winning goal that year, as well.

"He's what I call a third generation superstar," said hockey analyst Harry Neale. "Kids have now grown up emulating Paul Coffey, who had grown up emulating Bobby Orr."

The sad part of the Orr saga is that fans only had eight years to watch him at peak form. Knee problems limited him to 36 games from 1975 to 1979 and forced retirement at age 31.

Orr is now one of the top player agents in the business.

> "One thing I'm thankful for is I was never asked to change the way I played."
> – Bobby Orr

Bobby Orr wasn't even a teenager when he became the property of the Boston Bruins. Bruins fans had been hearing about Orr long before they saw him – needless to say he did not disappoint. He was rookie of the year in 1967 and won the Norris Trophy as best defenseman the following eight seasons.

Opponents Had Their Fill of Phil

Eight men have scored 70 or more goals in a single National Hockey League season, including Brett Hull with his booming shot, Wayne Gretzky getting 92 with élan and Jari Kurri via speed.

But there was little artistic finesse about Phil Esposito's climb to 76 goals. He would simply plant his physical bulk in the face of opposing goaltenders and dare defensemen to try to move his black-and-gold XXL hockey pants from the slot.

Few could do it, and that's why Espo was the first man to get above 70 and hold the record for 11 years before Gretzky and a batch of shooting stars came on the scene.

Ironically, it was a perceived lack of scoring that led Esposito to a rewarding career in Boston, with two Stanley Cups. Originally the property of the Blackhawks, and brought along the same chain as Bobby Hull, Esposito was sent to the sad-sack Bruins with Ken Hodge and Fred Stanfield in exchange for Pit Martin, Jack Norris and Gilles Marotte after Chicago lost to underdog Toronto in the 1967 Stanley Cup semifinals.

Within two years, Esposito was on the cusp of 50 goals, and he led the league in goals between 1969–70 and 1972–73. In between, there were two Stanley Cups, while the Blackhawks entered the 21st century with the league's longest championship drought.

"I coach a college team (in Fort Myers, Florida) and I still tell them to do the positional things Esposito did," said Don Awrey, his former Bruins teammate.

> **"Phil could stand in front of the net and control a game like the ace of a pitching staff."**
>
> – Don Awrey

Esposito wasn't only a scorer, he was a leader, a quality that came to life in the 1972 Summit Series between Canada and Russia. When the stunned Canadians were booed in Vancouver for falling behind 1–2–1 in the series, with four games in cold Moscow looming, a sweating, enraged Esposito went on national television to admonish the fans and urge them to get behind the downtrodden team.

Esposito picked up the torch in the next four games and helped Paul Henderson stage the most incredible comeback ever in the nation's international history. His NHL career finished with the Rangers in 1980–81, but he resurfaced 10 years later as a major force in the birth of the expansion Tampa Bay Lightning.

Underutilized by the Chicago Blackhawks, Esposito was dealt to the Boston Bruins and became a scoring sensation. After netting 35 goals in his first year with the Bruins, he exploded, scoring at least 40 goals in each of the next seven seasons.

Mr. Zero Was Chicago's Hero

There was only one thing wrong with the golden goaltending troika of Rogie Vachon, Gump Worsley and Tony Esposito — the Montreal Canadiens only had one net.

So after a 13-game cameo with the Habs in 1968–69, which included a 5–4–4 record, two shutouts and his name below Vachon and Worsley on the Stanley Cup, Esposito was dangled in the waiver draft, a gift from the hockey gods for some lucky team.

Enter the Chicago Blackhawks, who had won one playoff series since 1966, missed the playoffs completely in 1968–69 and needed an upgrade in net. They hit the jackpot in Esposito, who was, up until then, the lesser-known brother of the Boston Bruins' burly center Phil.

In the next seven seasons, Tony would record at least 30 wins and would twice lead the NHL in shutouts. In his first season in Chicago, he blanked the opposition 15 times, a feat accomplished by only three other goaltenders, all before 1930.

One of Esposito's biggest joys that year was playing in a 10–2 laugher against the Canadiens on the last night of the schedule. His old team needed the win to get in the playoffs, while Chicago finished first.

He was dubbed "Tony O" and "Mr. Zero" and was one of the first to popularize the butterfly style. His once awk-

> "When I joined the Blackhawks in the fall of 1969, we both had something to prove."
>
> – Tony Esposito

ward looking 35 became a number of choice for many young goalies.

"Being a goalie isn't complicated," he advised a young Richard Brodeur in the early 1980s. "Stay between the puck and the net."

He would win the Vezina Trophy three times between 1970 and 1974 and go on to 30-win seasons eight times and 423 total victories up until 1983–84. His goals-against average of 1.77 in 1971–72 would be the lowest mark for the next 17 NHL seasons.

But what Esposito couldn't do was lift the Hawks back into the winners circle, despite two trips to the Cup final in 1971 and 1973, both against new Habs goaltending savior Ken Dryden.

But the urge to out-do Phil never wavered, ever since the latter scored twice on him the first time he suited up against the Bruins. Twenty years later, the Tony Esposito–managed Pittsburgh Penguins would sweep Phil's New York Rangers out of the playoffs.

"I'm sure my father and mother are up there somewhere watching us," said Phil.

But the Espositos had helped Canada win the Summit Series in 1972. Tony had the only victory on home ice, a 4–1 decision at Maple Leaf Gardens, while Phil's leadership in Moscow helped secure the comeback.

Esposito's first full season in the NHL was a memorable one. He won the Calder Trophy as top rookie and the Vezina Trophy as top goalie, and he was named to the first All-Star Team.

The Unusual Case of Dryden vs. Dryden

In this age of saturation coverage of hockey, imagine the hype if two brothers were slated to play goal against each other for the first time in NHL history.

But the first meeting of the Dryden brothers on March 20, 1971, was not scheduled. Though Ken Dryden had been called up late in the season by the Montreal Canadiens and had noted an upcoming game against brother Dave and the Buffalo Sabres, he was advised not to get butterflies.

"[Canadiens coach] Al MacNeil told me a couple of days earlier that Rogie Vachon would start that game for us," Ken said. "I told Dad [Murray Dryden] not to bother coming. But he drove all the way from Toronto anyway."

Sabres coach Punch Imlach realized the potential significance of the game and posted Dave as his starting goaltender. Dave had been a great role model for Ken, diligently working his way through the minors for a shot at the NHL. Ken's rise had been more meteoric; he graduated right from Cornell University to the Habs.

When Ken didn't stay in for the anthems, Imlach replaced Dave with Joe Daley and Montreal headed towards an uneventful 5–2 win. But in the second period, Vachon went down with an injury. On the Habs bench, a nervous Dryden wondered why he wasn't getting up, until MacNeil leaned over and said "You're in."

Imlach wasted no time getting Dave in for Daley. Murray Dryden beamed in his seat at the Forum.

At the final siren, Ken thought about embracing Dave, but realized that as a rookie he shouldn't break the unwritten rule of on-ice fraternization. Dave had other ideas, parking himself at center ice so Ken would have to cross paths.

"We shook hands and a lot of people liked it," Ken said. "But over time, it became too distracting if we played against each other. You wanted your teammates to score, so I didn't enjoy it anymore."

Ken won the Conn Smythe Trophy that year, as Montreal won the Cup. He came back to fulfill his rookie eligibility for the Calder Memorial Trophy in 1971–72.

> "We were having a hamburger and kind of joked with each other, 'See you at center ice after we play tomorrow, ha, ha.'"
>
> – Dave Dryden

> "It was really one of those unbelievable things. Our dad, who took the chance of driving to Montreal when it made no sense, was rewarded."
>
> – Ken Dryden

After playing a career-high 53 games for the Sabres in 1973–74, Dave Dryden jumped to the WHA, where he would he would end up playing with a 17-year-old phenomenon named Wayne Gretzky.

Paul Henderson's Mission to Moscow

Canadian politicians can spend millions to promote national unity for the next 100 years. But they likely won't ever come close to the success that 20-odd hockey players and 3,000 fans had in a Moscow arena in September of 1972.

Given up for dead by many as the "Series of the Century" moved from shocking setbacks in Canada to the foreboding Russian capital, Team Canada dug their way from infamy to immortality.

"Henderson has scored for Canada!"

– Foster Hewitt

Paul Henderson, a little-known winger with the Maple Leafs, began the series overshadowed by Phil Esposito and other well-known stars of the NHL. But his line with Ron Ellis and Bobby Clarke was coach Harry Sinden's most dependable asset in the gruelling eight-game series.

Fighting disgruntled players in their own ranks and the unfamiliarity of the Soviet police state, and needing to win all three games after dropping the opener in Moscow, Team Canada and its hardy fans gave the Russians hell. Henderson scored the winners in Game 6 and 7, and after the Soviets took a 5–3 lead in the third period of Game 8, he capped the three-goal comeback with 34 seconds to play.

To this day, Henderson has no idea what seized him to order Peter Mahovlich off the ice so he could rendezvous with history. Foster Hewitt, himself a hockey legend behind the microphone, took it from there:

"Henderson took a wild stab at it and fell. There's another shot, right in front, he scores! Henderson has scored for Canada!"

The Moscow heroics changed his life forever, and at first he had a difficult time adjusting to the fame. But he's since used the experience to try and make a difference in the world.

"The goal gave me a chance to be a half-decent role model," he said. "My wife [Eleanor] and I have been able to raise money for charity." Henderson has raised thousands of dollars through the sale of '72-related memorabilia.

"I've had kids who weren't even born when I scored ask me for autographs for their dads. It's amazing. Maybe it has something to do with where our country is going. We want to define ourselves. For me, it has been a nice ride."

Canada looked full of ghost towns the afternoon of the final game. People who didn't watch at home went to bars or restaurants or the electronics department of major department stores, where there were banks of TVs.

"It was a series that was so anticipated, so surprising, so devastating and so triumphant — all at the same time," Canadian goaltender Ken Dryden said in 1999. "This was 27 days of full agony. It was 'us' against 'them' and we haven't really had anything the past few years like it. Maybe to bring out the best in us we need to have a 'them' come along again, whomever it be."

This remarkable eight-game series was the pinnacle of many of these great players' careers. Bobby Orr said, "What that team did, I don't think there has been a greater feat in sports. It was an unbelievable comeback against a great Russian team. I've never seen anything like it."

The League of Extraordinary Gentlemen

They were the good-time Charlies who crashed the party of stuffed shirts. They were the World Hockey Association, and more than a quarter century after its survivors merged with the NHL, the echo of those crazy days is still heard. The NHL would rue the day it laughed off the upstarts who broke the older league's contractual servitude monopoly and expanded to new markets in North America.

A 12-team league in a constant state of flux, the WHA's wobbly launch came on October 11, 1972, when the Ottawa Nationals hosted the Edmonton Oilers. Three teams had already changed cities by then, but the Canadian entries and those in the northern U.S. were well received.

Within the first few years of its existence, the WHA had lured names such as Bobby Hull, Gordie Howe, Howe's two sons and Dave Keon, and had exploited the rich European talent market ahead of the NHL. Those fringe players who had been unable to crack the NHL also relished the chance to play pro.

"It helped everyone associated with the game," four-year WHA veteran Ralph Backstrom said at a league reunion. "[Players], writers, GMs, coaches, trainers, broadcasters, everybody. It sent hockey in the same direction with regard to pay scale as football, baseball and basketball."

But in one six-week period, coach Harry Neale's Minnesota Fighting Saints made just one payday. "I could get them to play without pay, but not without meal money for the road," Neale recalled. "On one trip to Houston our team president got the money from some friends who owned bars, met us at the airport and tossed it to me in a shopping bag from about ten feet as the plane departed.

"(GM) Glen Sonmor and I had to count about $80 in piles of 20 for each player, one dollar bills, fives and twenties, which we balanced on our knees, on the seats and on top of the seats. The captain came back 20 minutes later and said 'a woman passenger had reported we might be bank robbers splitting loot. Thankfully, he was a hockey fan.'"

Teams such as Minnesota fought their way to respectability, the 1970s being the era of wanton fisticuffs. But clubs such as the Winnipeg Jets, who signed fluid Swedes Anders Hedberg and Ulf Nilsson, would have been more than a match for most NHL teams.

"We caused the NHL owners so many problems because it cost them twice as much to have players leave or stay," Neale said.

The NHL eventually realized neither league could win a prolonged war, and after two collapsed deals, a merger was arranged in time for the start of 1979–80 season. Edmonton, Winnipeg, Quebec and Hartford entered the NHL, while Birmingham and Cincinnati were paid to close shop.

> "The theory was, if you're going to be a mediocre team, be the toughest mediocre team in the league."
>
> – Harry Neale

The charismatic Bobby Hull brought much-needed attention to the WHA as it squared off against the NHL.

The Flower Blooms at the Forum

Like the lineage of great kings, the Montreal Canadiens always seemed to have someone ready to fill the superstars' skates.

Howie Morenz was not gone long before Rocket Richard arrived during the war years, and upon his retirement in 1960, Jean Beliveau led the team to six more Cups. On June 9, 1971, Beliveau announced he was leaving, and a day later the Habs drafted Guy Lafleur first overall with a pick obtained from the California Golden Seals.

It took a few years for the native of blue-collar Thurso, Quebec, to become acclimatized to the NHL, but once established on right wing, he tore up the circuit. With precision skating, a wicked shot and a mane of blond hair flowing behind him, "The Flower" was a six-time first-team All-Star in the latter half of the 1970s.

"I would say Lafleur didn't get as much credit as he should have for scoring big goals," his former coach Scotty Bowman said. "He got a lot of big goals for that team, especially the year we lost just eight games [1976–77]. We had a ton of one-goal games. Lafleur seemed to come through. He was the go-to guy and he came through."

In the season Bowman referred to, Lafleur had 80 assists and a league-high 136 points with linemates Steve Shutt

> **"[Guy Lafleur] didn't worry about defense. He didn't have to. The other teams shadowed him all the time."**
>
> – Scotty Bowman

and Jacques Lemaire. The Montreal Forum resonated with a long "Guuuuuy" whenever he touched the puck.

"The most underrated part of his game was his shot," Bowman insisted. "He could put a puck where he wanted. Most people say they remember him carrying the puck, stickhandling, going around guys. But I think it was Ken Dryden who said his shot is as sneaky as anyone he's seen."

Lafleur, whose salary never topped $400,000, sometimes wishes he could roll back the clock for the sake of the game.

"The players today are bigger than in my day and there are more good skaters on each team," he conceded. "But as soon as they get to the red line, they dump it in. I'd like to see one game where they didn't dump it in, just to see how good they really are. In my day, we controlled the puck, we didn't give it up. Now it's a chasing game."

Unlike Richard and Beliveau, retirement did not sit well with Lafleur. He was the franchise's all-time leading scorer, accepted his Hall of Fame laurels, tried business ventures and became a kind of ambassador for the team. But he came back in 1988 with the New York Rangers and scored twice in his Forum return that year. Two seasons back with the Quebec Nordiques rounded out his distinguished career.

The Canadiens knew exactly what they were getting when they drafted Lafleur first overall. He was coming off a season in which he had scored 130 goals in just 62 games playing for the Quebec Remparts of the QMJHL.

The Broad Street Bullies
Are Back in Town

At times they seemed more like an outlaw motorcycle gang than a hockey team. But the Philadelphia Flyers knew how to win, by talent, terror, guile, goaltending or some psychological ploy dreamed up by their canny coach, Freddy "The Fog" Shero.

In 1974 and 1975, they took the balance of power in the NHL from Original Six clubs such as Montreal, Boston and New York, becoming the first post-expansion team to win the Stanley Cup.

"We loved to go on the road and have the people hate us," forward Orest Kindrachuk told the *Toronto Sun.* "It made us play all that harder and fueled our desire. Our attitude was that it was our puck until someone came and took it."

With names like Dave "The Hammer" Schultz and Bob "Hound" Kelly, the Flyers could scare the hockey pants off many teams. The Spectrum, in which the team's record was 66–17–3, was as intimidating as the Roman Colosseum, especially when the Flyers used a recording of Kate Smith singing "God Bless America."

But the Flyers also had a 50-goal shooter in Rick MacLeish, a spiritual leader in Bobby Clarke, and, of course, Bernie Parent. The latter closed out Vezina Trophy and Conn Smythe Trophy years with Cup-clinching shutouts, beating the Boston Bruins 1–0 on May 19, 1974 and the Buffalo Sabres 2–0 on May 27 the following year.

"Win today and we walk together forever," Shero said as they went out to slay the Bruins.

"More true words were never spoken," defenseman Joe Watson said. "Here we are, 30 years after we won the Cup [the first of two straight] and there are 26 of us still living in the Philadelphia area, with an alumni that still stays in close contact."

That Flyer philosophy makes the franchise one of the NHL's tightest to this day.

"Our biggest desire was to succeed and that meant not letting a teammate down," Kindrachuk said. "If you had to block a shot, you did it, and if you weren't a fighter, you still fought."

The notoriously crusty fans in win-starved Philadelphia embraced the Flyers, both the stars and the sideshow. "Until we came along, Philadelphia was mostly known as a city of losing sports teams," Schultz said. "When we won the first Cup, it was a major event. Years later, people can tell you where they were on May 19, 1974.

"This is a tough sports town, but there is a saying. Win in Philadelphia and you'll be remembered forever. That's what happened with us."

> **"Win today and we walk together forever."**
>
> – Fred Shero

The 1974–75 edition of the Broad Street Bullies saw Dave Schultz rack up an NHL record 472 penalty minutes – nearly eight full games in the box.

Champagne on Ice: The Habs' New Year's Bash with the Red Army

You could have framed the game sheet of the New Year's Eve 1975 game between the Montreal Canadiens and the Central Red Army and created a timeless work of hockey art.

Called by some the greatest single international exhibition game, if not the best hockey game of all, the Montreal Forum match was played under unique conditions with spectacular results.

This was the Super Series '76 tour. The Red Army were the class of the Soviet League, with many of the stars of the '72 Summit Series still in their prime. The Habs were about to launch a dynasty that would win four straight Stanley Cups. And it was a goaltending rematch of Game 8 in Moscow in 1972, Vladislav Tretiak against Ken Dryden.

"The Red Army challenged us and we rose to the challenge," defenseman Larry Robinson said in his book. "I don't think I've ever seen the Canadiens skate, shoot, pass and check as we did in that game. I never wanted it to end."

Canadiens' coach Scotty Bowman began the game by pairing top defensive forward Bob Gainey with speedy sniper Guy Lafleur on the same line, which was a rarity. Montreal struck twice early in the first period on a high bullet drive by Steve Shutt.

> **"It brought back memories of how we used to play the game on a pond."**
>
> – Canadiens forward Peter Mahovlich

When Yvon Lambert put a five-hole rebound past Tretiak, the visitors seemed in over their heads. They were being outshot 7–0 and they were 0-for-2 on the power play. But this was the same arena where three years earlier, the Russian nationals had stumbled early and lulled Team Canada into complacency.

Boris Mikhailov got the Army on the board with a second-period wrist shot, and after an Yvan Cournoyer goal, the graceful Valeri Kharlamov stunned the crowd, slipping behind the defense for a beautiful backhand goal. Boris Alexanderov tied the game in the third period, setting up a wild finish filled with near-goals.

The game was fight-free, with both clubs showing a mutual respect rarely demonstrated in public.

"It was the greatest hockey in my career," Tretiak declared of his 35 saves, 16 in the third period, when a gang of future Hall of Fame Habs bombarded his goal.

Afterwards there was a wonderful photo-op at center ice of the game's three stars — Tretiak, Peter Mahovlich and Cournoyer. When an exhausted Mahovlich got into the interview studio with Howie Meeker, he apologized to viewers that Montreal hadn't beat the high-flying visitors, despite dominating them 38–16 on the shot clock.

"Don't apologize," Meeker responded. "It was the greatest entertainment in the world."

A participant of the 1972 Summit Series, Mahovlich relished any chance to skate with the Russians.

Canada Triumphs in the First Gathering of Hockey Clans

The creation of the 1976 Canada Cup was a trade-off; the top European nations agreed to come to a North American tournament every four years if Canada would cease its objection to playing in the annual world championships across the pond.

A powerful team was assembled by the host nation, led by the best of the two Stanley Cup powers of the day, the Montreal Canadiens and the Philadelphia Flyers. Also aboard were Bobby Orr and Bobby Hull, who had both missed the historic Summit Series four years earlier against the Soviets.

> **"Sittler's good because he listens to his coach. I told him to hang in there, fake the shot and you'll have an empty net."**
>
> – Don Cherry

It was the first chance for NHLers such as Sweden's Borje Salming to play for their native countries on this continent. But with the NHL's European talent explosion still a decade away, almost all the visiting nations were a mystery on this side of the Atlantic.

Most people predicted a Canada–Soviet final, especially when the red-and-white hosts hammered the Finns 11–2 to open the tournament and disposed of the Americans and Swedes. But the Czechoslovakians came in and rewrote the script.

Goaltender Vladimir Dzurilla threw up a wall to support Milan Novy's goal in a 1–0 preliminary round meeting that ended Canada's unbeaten run. Canada rallied to defeat the Soviets 3–1 in a must-win game for a rematch with the Czechoslovaks in the best-of-three final.

This time, the Canadians were ready for Dzurilla, chasing him from Game 1 with four goals in the first period. Game 2 in Montreal went to overtime, with Dzurilla in a relief role this time, replacing Jiri Holecek.

Acting on a tip from associate coach Don Cherry, Toronto's Darryl Sittler decided to hang on to the puck as he made a rush up the left side, waiting until Dzurilla came too far out to get back in position and sliding in the winner.

Bobby Orr was named tournament MVP, with two goals and seven assists, tying Viktor Zhluktov of the Soviets and teammate Denis Potvin for the tourney lead. But it was his last hurrah in the spotlight before knee problems ended his career.

For Sittler, it capped an incredible eight-month span in which he had a 10-point night (against Cherry's Bruins) and scored five goals in one playoff game versus the Flyers.

"The greatest highlight was the chance to play for my country," Sittler said at his Hall of Fame induction in 1989.

Despite his bad knees, Orr played like a man possessed. He tied Russian Victor Zhluktov for the tournament scoring lead and was named most valuable player.

Darryl's Night Was a Perfect 10

Don't expect Darryl Sittler to be yelling too loudly to restore wide-open hockey in the 21st century.

The more defensive the NHL becomes, the less chance his magical night of 10 points in one game will ever be matched or beaten.

For a generation of success-starved Leafs fans, February 7, 1976, brought a game that can't be topped, unless you count the Cup-clinching win. Six goals and four assists, never achieved before or since, even by Gretzky or Lemieux, or aided by a long line of sieves in nets that came with expansion.

In the wrong place at the wrong time was American-born Dave Reece, who was keeping the Boston Bruins' crease warm that night for the imminent return of Gerry Cheevers from the WHA. Reece had been told the night before that he was returning to the minors and was kept out late by a sympathetic Johnny Bucyk, which upset his pre-game preparations.

Sittler had two assists in the first period, then a hat trick in the second. The initial haul included a long five-hole slap shot and an assist as he came on during a delayed Boston penalty.

At that stage, Boston coach Don Cherry was looking down the bench at Cheevers, who caught Cherry's glance and threw a towel over his own head. Reece stayed in for the balance of the 11–4 laugher.

Another Sittler hat trick followed in the third period,

> *"It's about the only scoring record Wayne Gretzky doesn't have."*
>
> – Darryl Sittler

his ninth point, beating the existing NHL record held by Rocket Richard and Bert Olmstead. The tenth point was an improbable bank shot off Brad Park's skate from behind the Reece's net.

"Look at my face [on highlights] on the tenth point," Sittler said. "That smile and the shrug say it all. As much as people fault Reece, it was just a night when everything I shot and passed somehow found the way to the right place."

A slumping Sittler had just one goal in eight games before that night and had been severely criticized before the game by bombastic Toronto owner Harold Ballard.

"If we could find a center for Errol Thompson and Lanny McDonald we'd be dynamite," a snide Ballard had told the media.

Ballard wound up giving his captain a 200-year-old silver tea service in appreciation. But the sticks Sittler used, the pucks and the sweater he wore that night were all forgotten or misplaced. Nothing tangible remains, except the scoresheet.

Reece, who didn't play in the NHL after that season, went to work as admissions director at a school in Worcester, Massachusetts. To this day, he's never met Sittler face to face.

"Wouldn't you think he'd send me something, some little gift?" Reece said jokingly in 2001. "I helped put the guy in the Hall of Fame, and he put me in the Hall of Shame."

> "The thing I remember most about it is the ovation the fans gave me when I got my ninth point. That's something you just never forget." – Darryl Sittler

Saturday Night Fever: The Habs Dominate the Late 1970s

Two things took North America by storm in the late 1970s, disco and the Montreal Canadiens. From the drop of the puck in 1975–76, to carting off the last of four consecutive Stanley Cups in the spring of 1979, Montreal lost a grand total of 46 regular season games and just 10 in the playoffs.

"The Canadiens didn't just win, they dominated," said goaltender Ken Dryden. "They gave you no breathing room, no crack in their armor. It wasn't much fun for anybody else."

The man in charge was Scotty Bowman, with hockey's ultimate arsenal at his command. He had the game's best line of 60-goal men Guy Lafleur and Steve Shutt and gifted center Jacques Lemaire, relentless checkers such as Doug Jarvis and Bob Gainey, the latter described by admiring Russian national team coaches as the perfect hockey player.

Theirs was a defense that could fly around the rink like reckless Montreal taxi drivers, or hit like dump trucks. If you got past the big three, Larry Robinson, Serge Savard and Guy Lapointe, you still had to beat the lanky Dryden. The dressing room was a sportswriter's dream, accommodating players who had unique insights into the game that would serve them well later as coaches, managers and executives.

"If you ask me about the best team I coached to the Cup, I'd have to say it was the '76–77 team," Bowman said upon retiring in 2002. "That team had the likes of Lafleur, Robinson, Shutt and Dryden, all of whom started to blossom at once."

Part of the success of the Canadiens stemmed from their ability to weather the arrival of the WHA better than clubs such as their arch-rivals from Toronto. But General Manager Sam Pollock and Bowman were always tinkering, particularly with the first Cup team. The 1976 Habs had to break the brawny Philadelphia Flyers' two-year hold on the title, giving back a little of the Flyers' own intimidation medicine along the way.

Next came the great 1976–77 campaign, in which Montreal allowed just 171 regular season goals and blew away Boston 4–0 in the final.

Another win over Don Cherry's Bruins followed in 1978. Just as the Bruins tied the series 2–2, Bowman pulled Pierre Larouche, Pierre Mondou and Mario Tremblay out of the press box and won the next two games. Robinson had 17 assists in the series and won the Conn Smythe Trophy.

The fourth and final Cup was said to be aided by the famous Forum ghosts, who caused the Bruins to have a too-many-men penalty with a semifinal series victory in sight.

"But you never felt you could depend on destiny," Dryden said. "You had to create it."

> "I look at the pictures of those teams and see nine Hall of Famers, not including Scotty Bowman and Sam Pollock. Some nights you were thinking, 'I don't want to play against these guys, I want to get them to sign my stick'."
>
> – ex-Bruin Peter McNab

| Cournoyer, Lafleur and Robinson were three of the nine players from the 1976–77 Canadiens who made their way into the Hockey Hall of Fame.

The Buffalo Sabres' French Connection

Contrary to popular belief, Quebec's most dynamic hockey players didn't all wind up wearing the uniform of the Montreal Canadiens or the Quebec Nordiques.

The Buffalo Sabres boasted perhaps the best line from La Belle Province in the early 1970s, with Gilbert Perreault at center, Rick Martin on the left and Rene Robert on the right.

Perreault and Martin were drafted in consecutive years from the Montreal Junior Canadiens. Robert, from Trois-Rivières, Quebec, was chased three times by Punch Imlach.

While still with the Maple Leafs in 1968, Imlach signed Robert to their farm team, but then was fired. As the Sabres' first GM, he tried for Robert in the 1971 waiver draft, but the Pittsburgh Penguins put in a counterclaim. Imlach eventually traded hockey's clown prince, Eddie Shack, to the Pens to get Robert late in 1971–72, and the next season, the Connection bloomed.

"Rick was a great shooter and scorer, Rene had a great feel for the game," Perreault said. "We were criss-crossing, there was a lot of European influences. It was a great time."

Between the three, they garnered six first or second-team All-Star nominations between 1973–74 and 1976–77.

> "Punch Imlach knew that getting the right blend of three French-Canadian guys would click."
>
> – Gilbert Perreault

All three wound up among the NHL's top 10 scorers in 1974–75. Perreault would finish with 1,326 points in 1,191 games.

The line was at its zenith in 1975, as the Sabres overcame the Canadiens in the playoffs and attempted to knock off the defending Cup champs Philadelphia.

The series is best remembered for the fog banks that enveloped the auditorium in a late-May heat wave. In a comic attempt to break up the soup, time was called and arena attendants donned blades and waved around big towels and sheets. Martin had six points in six games, but the Flyers held Perreault and Robert to a goal each.

The Connection would have never connected had Buffalo not won a wheel-of-fortune spin on June 11, 1970, at the NHL draft. The expansion Sabres and Vancouver Canucks chose numbers above and below 11 for the right to pick first overall and when the spin had apparently stopped at one, the Canucks began celebrating.

But Imlach pointed out it was actually resting on 11 and the Sabres quickly chose Perreault and left another Quebecois, defenseman Dale Tallon, for Vancouver. Tallon was talented, but played just three years in Vancouver before going to Chicago.

Perreault, Martin and Robert combined for 131 goals and 291 points during their outstanding '74–75 campaign.

The Class of '79

In hockey's crapshoot world of amateur drafting, the class of 1979 remains the most remarkable group ever to graduate.

From No. 1 pick Rob Ramage of the Colorado Rockies to No. 21 Kevin Lowe, everyone chosen that June had a noteworthy NHL career.

"A lot of us had played [for Canada] in the world junior tournament for the two years previous, so you knew it was going to be a good crop," said winger Rick Vaive of the Sherbrooke, Quebec, Canadians, who went fifth overall to the Vancouver Canucks. "There were a few guys who went on to get 400 goals, such as Michel Goulet." Goulet was chosen 20th by the Quebec Nordiques from his hometown Remparts.

The start of 1979–80 saw the NHL absorb the four remaining teams from the World Hockey Association, which had allowed players such as Vaive and Mike Gartner to jump to the pros a year earlier. But what really distinguishes this group is their scoring feats and eventual admission to the Hall of Fame.

The pack included eight defensemen, with Ramage, Ray Bourque, Kevin Lowe and Craig Hartsburg among them. The first of 10 wingers was Mike Foligno of the Sudbury Wolves and right behind him, Gartner, who would set an NHL record for most 30-goal seasons. Portland Winter Hawks center Perry Turnbull went second behind Ramage, and though he's among the least known of the group, he played nine solid seasons with St. Louis, Montreal and Winnipeg.

The Brandon Wheat Kings of the Western Hockey League contributed three players to the round, forwards Laurie Boschman, Brian Propp and defenseman Brad McCrimmon.

Wayne Gretzky entered the NHL that year as a protected player of the Edmonton Oilers, or he would've been the easy first pick.

"I remember the draft took a long time to complete that day," Vaive said. "Because the four new teams came in, they conducted the whole thing by phone. The only bad thing is that I don't have that picture every other junior has on draft day of being presented with a team sweater."

The class of '79 also produced a number of future coaches, general managers and player union executives.

"We'll all bump into each other from time to time," Vaive said. "We realize we were part of something special."

The second round also featured some well-known picks, such as Mark Messier, Neal Broten, Glenn Anderson, Dale Hunter, Anton Stastny and Thomas Steen.

> **"All 21 of us made the NHL. With the league so big now, I don't know if there will ever be another first round draft like it."**
>
> – Rick Vaive

Ray Bourque (No. 14) was one of five players from the '79 draft who went on to score at least 400 goals in his career. The others were, Gartner, Vaive, Goulet and Propp.

The New Centurions, 1980–2004

America's Finest Hour

To understand why the Americans' gold medal in the 1980 Olympics was so meaningful, you need to look at the political map of the day.

The Russians were as large on the world stage as in the hockey arena, with the invasion of Afghanistan on everyone's mind and relations strained with the United States. America was also feeling the humiliation of its embassy staff being held hostage in Iran, sparking great unrest from coast to coast.

What better remedy than a group of fresh-faced school boys bettering the robotic Russians on the blackboard and refusing to be out-worked?

"I wanted my players to see that the Soviets were mortal," coach Herb Brooks said, in meticulously readying the team for a date with the Big Red Machine. He wanted a hybrid hockey team, that had the pluck of the Canadians and the execution of the Soviets.

Al Michaels's famous cry from the press box at a little arena in Lake Placid, New York, on February 22, 1980, came as the seconds ticked down in a 4–3 win over the Russians, one of six games in the tournament that the U.S. had trailed in and won. The Americans wrapped up the gold against Finland two days later.

"Do you believe in miracles?"

–broadcaster Al Michaels

But was it all really a miracle?

"There was a certain portrayal that we were a bunch of college kids who got together, drove out to Lake Placid in a van and won a gold medal," back-up goaltender Steve Janaszak said. "There was never enough appreciation of the talent level of players such as Mike Ramsey and Ken Morrow."

Brooks, dismissed by many in the game as a madman and by others as a genius, squeezed everything he had from his players. His motivational methods went unappreciated until well after the gold-medal game against the Finns made them household names in a grateful nation.

The Miracle on Ice electrified the nation and would inspire a new generation of American players to take up the game, from traditional hotbeds in Minnesota and Massachusetts to beyond. It helped pave the way for a World Cup win in 1996, a women's gold medal in 1998 and a world junior hockey championship in 2003.

A new movie on the subject called *Miracle* opened in 2004. Tragically, Brooks had died in a car accident the year before.

■ Fifteen members of this historic team went on to play in the NHL.

These Three Kings
Have Traveled Afar

Had Wayne Gretzky broken in with Los Angeles in 1979–80 and not the Edmonton Oilers, he might have had trouble making the Kings' first line.

That was the year a prolific trio of purple and gold was assembled, dubbed the Triple Crown Line, that went on to produce big numbers in the early part of the 1980s.

Marcel Dionne, destined to become a Hall of Famer and a top-five NHL career scorer with 1,771 points, was the unit's creative force, with rugged Dave Taylor on the right and Charlie Simmer on the left.

"It was like art out there, the way we scored goals."

– Marcel Dionne

The diminutive Dionne started his career in grand fashion with Detroit in 1971, but became the Kings' first true superstar when traded west four years later. He led the Kings in scoring nine times and had five consecutive 50-goal seasons.

Taylor, picked 210th overall the year Dionne arrived, developed quickly and had 91 points in 1978–79. He became one of the most popular athletes in L.A., overcoming a stuttering problem and doing many charitable acts.

"Most people don't know how great a player he was," ex-King Mike Murphy said. "When Mike Bossy was having all those great 50-goal seasons, very quietly Taylor was the best right winger in hockey. He could score, he was tough, he fought, he did everything."

Simmer was another unlikely find. He'd played for the rival California Golden Seals and was never far removed from the minor league buses. When placed with Dionne and Taylor in 1979–80, he promptly led the NHL with 56 goals.

But there wasn't the supporting cast to take the Kings to the heights attained by the powerhouse teams of the day, the Montreal Canadiens, the New York Islanders and the Oilers. Long before blanket television coverage brought most west coast games to eastern viewers, some of the Triple Crown Line's best feats were accomplished in anonymity, seen only in the box scores of the next day's newspaper.

Simmer was traded to Boston at the start of the 1984–85 season, and retired in 1988, later joining the electronic media. Dionne moved to the New York Rangers in 1987, tagged as one of the greatest forwards in the NHL never to win a Cup.

"I've watched guys win two or three Cups that were fourth-liners," Dionne once observed. "They probably wouldn't have made the Kings."

Today he lives in western New York, operating a sports memorabilia business, among others.

Taylor hung in with the Kings the longest of the three and was rewarded in his 16th season when the Gretzky-led team, now clad in black and silver, went to the Cup final. He dedicated the feat to his retired colleagues, but the Kings lost to the Canadiens, whose ranks included Dionne's younger brother Gilbert. Taylor has been the Kings' general manager since 1997.

❚ The best season for this trio was 1980–81, when they combined for 161 goals and 352 points.

The Year the Flyers
Forgot How to Lose

Very little was expected of the 1979–80 Philadelphia Flyers when the season started, let alone a 35-game undefeated streak.

"It was a team in transition, which is why I got the job in the first place," said coach Pat Quinn, who was just starting his first full season in the business.

The Flyers began adjusting to a new decade in which their Broad Street antics had become outdated. They had been looking for new coaching blood midway through the previous year, and Quinn had given up on trying to get a foothold in the business world. Flyers' management looked at 1979–80 as a rebuilding year and was hardly prepared for what followed.

The club opened on October 14, 1979, defeating the Maple Leafs 4–3 at the Spectrum. By December 22, they were heading into Boston and had yet to lose, challenging a League record of 29 games undefeated. They put away the B's in a rink that always gave them problems.

By January 6, 1980, with a 4–2 victory at Memorial Auditorium in Buffalo, the Flyers had compiled 25 wins and 10 ties. It was the longest such streak in professional sports history. But they lost 7–2 the next night in Minnesota.

"There was no escaping that one, we didn't take them

> **"The foot soldiers did a remarkable job, our veterans could change a game, we had guys on defense no one even heard of. The record was truly a team effort."**
>
> – Pat Quinn

seriously," Quinn said with a laugh. "But it was a good run."

Quinn was quick to credit stars such as Bob Clarke, Reggie Leach, Bill Barber and goaltender Pete Peeters, but saved the lion's share of praise for sluggo defensemen Frank Bathe, Norm Barnes and Mike Busniuk, three of the nine minor-leaguers he employed that year.

"I'd never have played in the NHL without Pat," said Busniuk. "We were treated like men. You made a mistake, he put you back on the ice. You missed curfew, he didn't say a word, but you knew to work extra hard at practice the next day. Even when he sent me down, he looked me in the eye."

Quinn won the Jack Adams Trophy as coach of the year that season. Barber, later to win that award himself with the Flyers, said Quinn had a significant influence on his career that season.

"I really admired him for the job he did that year," Barber said. "He was open with his communication and showed a lot of tolerance and patience."

Quinn's Flyers ended with a record of 48–12–20 and took the New York Islanders to a seventh game in the Cup final, but lost.

Pete Peeters, who shared the goaltending duties with Phil Myre, finished the season with 29 wins versus just five losses.

When Fantasy Island Became a Reality

The New York Islanders' first Stanley Cup was a long time in the making, but they got the hang of winning very quickly.

From the spring of 1975, when they'd battled to within a victory of going to the final, the Isles were knocking on the door of greatness, with four trips to the semifinals.

The 1980 playoffs provided their first of four titles as the club painstakingly built by Bill Torrey and Al Arbour took off on the longest consecutive Cup run by an American team in NHL history. Mike Bossy, Bryan Trottier and Clark Gillies were joined by newcomers Butch Goring and Ken Morrow.

The first title came in dramatic fashion, with a Game 6 overtime win over the Philadelphia Flyers, an incredible Bob Nystrom deflection at the poetically lucky time of 7:11.

"Being a Montreal boy with my name on the Stanley Cup was the greatest," Bossy wrote in his autobiography. "I could only think of one thing better. Another Cup."

The next two championships came at the expense of ruining two Cinderella stories. The Minnesota North Stars made it to their first final, but could only steal a game against New York. The Vancouver Canucks suffered the same fate in 1982, unable to slow down the Isles' mix of scoring and airtight defense, failing to win once.

Bossy had 17 goals against all teams in the 1982 playoffs, five of them game-winners. His seven goals in the final earned him the Conn Smythe Trophy. Arbour said his players' self-imposed "accountability" made them a joy for him to coach and so hard to play against.

"The veterans — Trottier, Gillies, Potvin, Tonelli — they all made sure new guys adhered," Arbour said. "No one went babbling to the press with complaints. It all stayed in the room."

The Isles fended off one challenge by the up-and-coming Edmonton Oilers, winning their fourth title in a year everyone wrote them off as past their prime. But they reluctantly handed over the Cup in 1984, with the Oilers having learned their lesson.

"When I lined up for the post-series handshakes, I looked into the eyes of every Oiler and recognized the joy," Bossy said. "I've never forgotten what it was like to win for the first time."

The Isles have not been back to the final to date.

> **"Until that moment, we were considered a team of losers and chokers. If Nystrom doesn't score, who knows what happens to our team?"**
>
> – Al Arbour

Bob Nystrom on his Cup-winning goal, "I really didn't think it was going to go in. I never scored a goal on my backhand all year. I had to get it high, and sure enough, it went high."

Gartner Gave Back to the Game

When Alf Gartner knocked out the back of the family's garage to build a poolroom, he found about 30 pucks stuck in the drywall. The culprit had to be his teenage son Mike, but considering where the trail led, to the Hockey Hall of Fame with 708 goals, it was a small price to play. Mike also admitted he had probably smashed a few windows and dented the side of the suburban Toronto house along the way.

"I would never consider myself a superstar," Gartner said. "But I was in the league for a long period of time and I'd like to think that I always maintained a consistency as a good player."

Gartner's 33 goals for the OHA's Niagara Falls Flyers in 1976–77 was an omen. In 1978–79 with the Cincinnati Stingers, he dueled Wayne Gretzky for WHA rookie of the year honors. The fourth pick overall in an expanded NHL in 1979, he set to work with 36 goals for the Washington Capitals, a pace that did not abate for 16 years, until the shortened 1994–95 schedule.

"His accuracy is incredible," former NHL goaltender Pete Peeters said. "He's made a living shooting at the five-hole. He's so patient, he waits for the opening and then you're dead."

Speed was another part of the Gartner arsenal. He continued to win NHL fastest skater competitions well after his 30th birthday. "The belief that when you turn 30 and suddenly are too old for pro sports is falling by the wayside," Gartner said in the late 1990s.

He avoided serious injury his whole career, and when he did hit a slump, wife Colleen would send him to the TV room, where Gartner had a highlight tape of his best goals. An hour or so of viewing usually fixed the problem. Gartner would get 30 goals in each of a total of 17 seasons, another record.

He played for Washington, the Minnesota North Stars, the New York Rangers, Toronto and Phoenix. Gretzky's first NHL goal came against Glen Hanlon and, coincidentally, Gartner's 100th, 200th and 300th were against the same man. Gartner's 500th was against Mike Liut, his one-time teammate on the Stingers.

A religious man, the father of three was one of the classiest men in the sport, and still holds an executive position with the NHL Players' Association.

> "I was a man playing a boy's game until the age of 38 and I had a great time doing it."
>
> – Mike Gartner

A sniper from the outset, Gartner scored at least 30 goals in each of his first 15 seasons, a record unlikely to be broken.

Too Young, Too Fast: The Death of Pelle Lindbergh

Twenty years have passed since Pelle Lindbergh died tragically in a car accident, yet the Philadelphia Flyers of that era still have a hard time believing it. The Swedish stopper had so much going for him, having won the 1984–85 Vezina Trophy and off to a start of 6–2 the following season.

It ended when his Porsche 930 smashed into the front of a schoolhouse in suburban New Jersey, not far from where he'd attended a team function that night. He was 26.

"You think back to yourself, 'What could I have done?'" teammate Brad Marsh said. "But I realize there wasn't anything I could have done. The way he drove that night was the way he always drove. No difference. He had that car and he was proud of it."

Lindbergh had already won over any Flyers skeptical of a European goaltender by playing a solid season for their Maine Mariners farm team. As a Flyer, he was 87–49–15, and he won the Vezina Trophy with 40 wins in 65 starts.

Lindbergh loved to imitate various goaltending characteristics of Flyers icon Bernie Parent. He even copied his mask design. Marsh named his son Erik after Lindbergh's full first name.

> **"Who knows what would have happened if he'd stayed alive? He was developing into one of the best goaltenders in the league."**
>
> – Brian Propp

"Some people name them for their fathers, some name them for themselves," Marsh said. "We tossed around a million names but we wanted to name him after someone we really respected. It seemed the right thing to do."

Lindbergh and the Flyers were celebrating a win and a five-day layoff when he was killed. Police reported that Lindbergh was legally drunk at the time of the accident, though Marsh, Brian Propp and others said it was out of character. They believe he was just unfamiliar with the road he chose near the Flyers practice facility.

"It was pure shock for everyone," Propp said. "He very rarely had more than two beers. The alcohol was not the big story everyone made it out to be.

"Dave Poulin gave such a moving eulogy at his service. It was tough to move on from that. The Flyers have had so much tragedy in the past 25 years with the deaths of Lindbergh, Barry Ashbee [from leukemia], Dimitri Tertyshny [a boating accident] and Bill Barber's wife [cancer]."

Bobby Clarke said of the tragedy, "It's not what it does to the organization, the organization will survive. It's what it does to the family, to the teammates. We all lost a great young man in Pelle Lindbergh."

Black Gold: Edmonton's Fifth Cup in Seven Years

By 1990, seeing the Edmonton Oilers win the Stanley Cup was not news. But doing it without Wayne Gretzky certainly qualified as a man-bites-dog story.

For the Oilers and their fans, this last of five Cups in seven years, and sixth appearance in eight years, was one of the sweetest. Many observers thought the dynasty had ended the previous season when the Calgary Flames emerged as champions the same year Gretzky was traded to the Los Angeles Kings.

Money goaltender Grant Fuhr was out of the lineup, and also gone, traded to Pittsburgh, was All-Star defenseman Paul Coffey, a prelude to the flood of stars leaving the cash-strapped team. The coaching reins were in John Muckler's hands, with Glen Sather devoting his time to executive duties.

But Edmonton had the talent to make the playoffs and survive a 3–1 deficit in its opening series against the Winnipeg Jets, plus a second playoff triumph over Gretzky and the Kings. The Oilers also briefly trailed in the Western Conference championship against the Chicago Blackhawks before arriving in familiar surroundings in the Cup final.

> **"We just stepped into another era."**
> – Kevin Lowe

"This year, it's extra-special," declared Mark Messier. "These kids came so far, so fast."

He was referring to the youthful line of Martin Gelinas, Adam Graves and Joe Murphy, who had been together just three games before the playoffs had got underway.

The series against Boston kicked off with the longest game in Cup final history, a 115-minute, 13-second overtime seesaw, finally won in the wee hours by Petr Klima's goal. The Bruins never recovered from that, and the series was over in five games.

Messier, now wearing the captain's C, took the Cup for a victory lap around Boston Garden with alternates Lowe and Jari Kurri. In Fuhr's place, the unheralded Bill Ranford won the Conn Smythe Trophy with a playoff record of 16–6.

"This one is for the G-Man," defenseman Kevin Lowe said. "Wayne was a big part of our lives. He was a big part of this whole thing. We followed on his coattails and developed our pride, our abilities and our winning attitudes. This was like winning it for the first time all over again."

The names of Lowe, Messier, Fuhr, Glenn Anderson, Randy Gregg, Charlie Huddy and Jari Kurri appeared on all five Oilers Cups.

The post-Gretzky era allowed Mark Messier to take control of the now seasoned Oiler team. In his finest season as a pro, he won the Hart Trophy as league MVP.

Alberta Anguish: Gretzky Goes South for a Kings' Ransom

Everyone in Edmonton remembers the day their hockey team's oil-drop logo became a huge teardrop.

Wayne Gretzky has been traded, and although time would show that the Oilers wouldn't fade in his absence, they would never be whole again, either.

"The emotions we're dealing with here are not unlike those of a death in the family," wrote Terry Jones in the *Edmonton Sun.* "A death not by natural causes."

No hint of such a blockbuster deal was in the air in that summer of 1988. The Oilers had just won their fourth straight Cup. Gretzky had taken the Conn Smythe with 43 points in 18 games. He was married to actress Janet Jones on July 16 in what was called Canada's royal wedding. He had every intention of living his life in Edmonton as an Oiler. But events behind the scenes had gathered steam.

Owner Peter Pocklington entertained thoughts of trading Gretzky to Vancouver only a day after the Cup was won. Gretzky refused and the rumors quieted, until the Los Angeles Kings and high-roller owner Bruce McNall got involved. Pocklington okayed a trade as long as

> **"It's the hardest thing I've ever been through. I don't think there's an August 9th where I haven't thought about it."**
> – Wayne Gretzky

McNall could convince Gretzky to leave, and No. 99 was mad enough at Pocklington at the time to say yes. His 1,669 points and eight Hart Trophies were changing addresses.

Gretzky joined the Kings along with Marty McSorley (a personal request) and Mike Krushelnyski in exchange for Martin Gelinas, Jimmy Carson, three first-round picks and cash. Edmonton would go on to win another Cup in 1990 before all of its free-agent assets were stripped by big spending teams.

For Gretzky, what began as a journey to the unknown with the Kings turned out to have a major impact on the face of the NHL. He brought the fans back to a major market, within three wins of the 1993 Cup, and convinced entrepreneurs in Anaheim and San Jose that hockey could fly in southern California.

Many have attributed the sport's explosion in the 1990s in the entire U.S. Sun Belt — both NHL and minor league — to events of August 9, 1988. But the people in Edmonton took little solace in that.

"I know we would have won more than one more Cup, probably two or three," lamented GM Glen Sather. "We were too good at that point."

Gretzky played eight seasons in Los Angeles but was unable to lead his team to a Stanley Cup. In fact, his Kings only once made it past the second round of the playoffs.

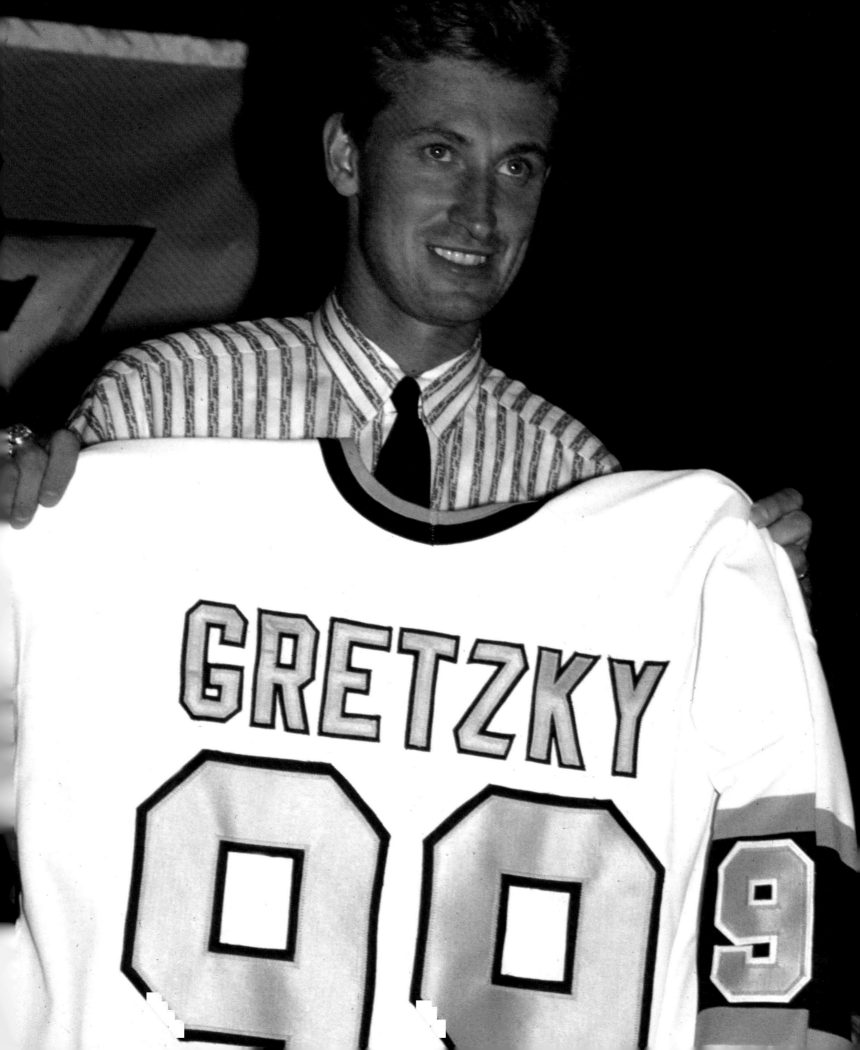

A Mark of Excellence
Nears the End of the Road

In another life, Mark Messier said, he could have been Rolling Stones' front man Mick Jagger — and he would have been very good at it.

But he did quite well in his chosen profession, wielding a hockey stick instead of a microphone, creating some gold records and bringing the arena crowds to their feet.

He is known in the hockey lexicon as Moose or Mess, and to these we can now add Methuselah, for he has spent 25 seasons in the league after the 2003–04 season, one short of Gordie Howe's record. In that span, he's been a six-time Stanley Cup winner, a charter member of the Edmonton Oilers dynasty and the captain who "guaranteed" the playoff success that ended the New York Rangers' 54-year Cup curse.

Even though he's missed the playoffs since 1997, he's comfortably in second place in NHL post-season scoring with 295 points, second only to old pal Wayne Gretzky.

The last playing link to the World Hockey Association could still be around when teenage phenom Sidney Crosby arrives in a couple of years, but the 2003–04 season might turn out to be Messier's last. He's no charity case, with 43 points in 76 games for the Rangers in

> **"To be a rock'n'roll star and have the fans go crazy. Would that be a rush or what?"**
>
> – Mark Messier

2003–04, to finish third on the team. But he's considering a graceful exit.

Compare that to his debut season, when he jabbed his stick menacingly in the face of Montreal Canadiens future Hall of Famer Larry Robinson in the 1981 playoffs.

"I don't suppose it would be the politically right thing to do now, but at the time it seemed like it was," Messier recalled.

Years later, Messier would bowl over Gretzky in a game between the Oilers and Gretzky's new team, the Los Angeles Kings, a move that cured the Oilers of giving too much respect to their former star.

Mentor Glen Sather made a slight correction to Messier's game in his formative years, advising him to augment his unpredictable slap shot in favor of a wrist shot. That's since translated to almost 1,900 career points. Messier passed Gordie Howe for second place in NHL scoring in 2003–04.

"I have a tremendous amount of respect for Gordie," Messier said. "I think [my staying power] is just due to longevity, good fortune and tremendous people around me. [Catching Howe] wasn't something I set out to do."

With a career for the ages, Messier won two Hart Trophies, a Conn Smythe Trophy and was an All-Star 14 times during his 25 NHL seasons.

Mario's Magnificent Comeback(s)

Super Mario never tires of encores. Thought to be finished many times in his storied NHL career, Lemieux made three dramatic comebacks, one from cancer, one from back pains and the last from the executive office of the Pittsburgh Penguins, where he decided to become the first player/owner in the game.

Though his future is once again in doubt as the 2004–05 season approaches, the Pens haven't bothered putting his retired number 66 back in the rafters.

He'd missed three and a half seasons in December of 2000, and the memory of back-to-back titles for Pittsburgh in 1991 and 1992 was fading along with the current team's hopes. But he summoned his front-office staff to his office to announce that a new player was coming into the line-up. He kept a straight face as they tried to guess if he'd made a trade or signed a free agent. No one had an inkling he was planning a return when he innocently asked the trainers for an exercise bike to prepare for an old-timers' game early in 2001.

The news had a rejuvenating effect on the team. On the night of his return, December 27, the Mellon Arena roof was lit up with a giant 66 as if summoning a super hero.

> **"It's hard to figure how we could be so lifeless before and so confident now. But a player like Mario can make that difference."**
>
> – Jaromir Jagr

Media requests came from as far away as Tokyo. Lemieux picked up a point on his first shift against the Toronto Maple Leafs, prompting Wayne Gretzky to call and leave a message inviting him to play for the 2002 Canadian Olympic team. That season, Lemieux scored 76 points in his remaining 43 games.

He'd had a similar experience on March 2, 1993, in a game the *Pittsburgh Post Gazette* ranked No. 1 in a list of 10 memorable Mario games. That was a night when Lemieux had just a goal and an assist in a 5–4 loss in Philadelphia, a relatively meaningless regular-season game. But it was a match he'd played just hours after receiving his final radiation treatment for Hodgkin's Disease.

Weak from the treatment, he put on a turtleneck to hide the scars and made it to a plane that whisked him across the state to play in Philadelphia that night.

"It's crazy," teammate Kevin Stevens said. "Can you even imagine what he did tonight? There's only one person in the world who could do it. And it's him."

A sign in the stands, paraphrasing the famous credit card ad, read: "Beer, $5. Ticket, $500. Watching Mario Lemieux return, priceless."

A remarkable talent, had Lemieux been healthy throughout his career, he likely would have challenged Wayne Gretzky's scoring records.

For these Hardworking Habs, Overtime Paid Off in Silver

In the spring of 1993, the Canadiens made overtime party time. Eleven times they went to an extra period and won the final 10, en route to capturing their 23rd Stanley Cup to date. But as you can guess, such a high-wire act is not without danger.

The Habs lost an early game in their opening round series to the Quebec Nordiques in the extra period, and there were fears that goaltender Patrick Roy and company would be a quick kill.

But five nights later, Vince Damphousse was the hero at 10:30 of overtime, and the pattern was set. Kirk Muller clinched the series with his winning goal, and the Habs shuffled off to Buffalo.

The stunned Sabres lost three overtimes in that series, all by 4–3 counts, on goals by Guy Carbonneau, Gilbert Dionne and Muller, the last taking until 11:37 to complete. The next test, against the New York Islanders, required double overtime. Stephan Lebeau ended it at 26:21, the longest of the ten games and once more a 4–3 score.

"It's not an easy way to do it," coach Jacques Demers said. "It's tough on everybody, but it's great when you win."

> **"Without being cocky, when it comes to overtime we just feel we can win."**
> – Montreal coach Jacques Demers

Two nights after Lebeau's heroics, the hard-checking Carbonneau took his turn in the spotlight. His goal eked out a 2–1 win and put the Habs in the driver's seat to go to the final against the Los Angeles Kings.

L.A. took the first game in regulation and was less than two minutes away from another win when Marty McSorley was caught with an illegal stick. That begat a series of misfortunes for the Western Conference champions.

The next three games went to Montreal, all in overtime, two of them settled in the first minute — two in which Montreal had a regulation lead of two or more goals. In Game 5, John LeClair used Darryl Sydor of the Kings to knock it in his own goal on a two-on-one, getting his second overtime goal in as many games.

To date, the Habs have not lost an overtime game in the final since 1978, and their 10 wins, six on the road, are league records.

"We're at a loss for words," Kings captain Wayne Gretzky said after Game 5. The Canadiens won the sixth game clincher 4–1 without the need of sudden death.

"I'm so proud of this team," Demers said. "There were so many favorites, but we never stopped believing. We were like the boxer who didn't want to go down."

Unlike the high-flying Montreal teams of the past, the '92–93 Habs relied on hard work and a little bit of luck to get the job done.

Surviving the Madhouse on Madison

In the 1989 playoffs between the Chicago Blackhawks and the Calgary Flames, the din inside the Madhouse on Madison was recorded at 130 decibels.

"It is past the pain threshold," the Hawks' Trent Yawney said. "The glass was shaking."

That is typical of the war stories that survive 10 years after the Chicago Stadium was demolished. It was the loudest rink in the NHL, one fact on which players, management, officials, fans and media all agreed.

Stanley Cups have eluded the Blackhawks since 1961, but that didn't stop loyal fans from cramming into the old building, with its booming pipe organ and low roof that trapped the sound of 17,250 people. Everyone made sure to get there early, so as not to miss Wayne Messmer's famous rendition of "The Star Spangled Banner," known as "the loudest two minutes in sports."

The cheering would begin on the first note and drown him out by the time he got to the "the home of the brave."

"At first, as a performer, it bothered me," Messmer said. "But the more I thought about it, the more I felt it was appropriate. Basically, it's a war song and Chicago is a blue-collar city. It fits."

> "If your heart wasn't pumping by the time you made it [to ice level] then you weren't alive."
>
> – referee Bryan Lewis

Visiting players went stir-crazy on the bench trying to remain at attention during the ruckus. As for the Hawks, no matter what the caliber of their team, they plugged into the manic energy, came out hitting and made the opening 10 minutes a challenge for any visitors. "It was great to work there, because the crowd wouldn't let your mind get out of the game," referee Bryan Lewis said.

In February 1990, the Stadium played a starring role in a worldwide broadcast. The NHL All-Stars were in town, just as the invasion of Kuwait had put the U.S. at war with Iraq. With no baseball or football on national television that week to blow off steam, patriotic patrons covered the Stadium in red, white and blue and almost blew the roof off.

"You felt like joining the army," said Flames director of hockey operations Al MacNeil.

Vince Damphousse of the Maple Leafs scored four goals that day. The Leafs figured prominently in the closing of the Stadium in 1994, playing the last regular season game there. Mike Gartner had the only goal in a 1–0 playoff win that closed the building for good.

"I won't be afraid to cry," Hawks great Stan Mikita said of the Stadium's send-off.

After making it to the post-season in 35 of their final 36 seasons at Chicago Stadium, the Blackhawks have struggled in their new home, the United Center, missing the playoffs in six of 10 seasons.

Blazing a Trail to Three Memorial Cups

Building a junior hockey dynasty is tough in the modern era, when the clubs are subject to everything from economics to rival leagues.

But the Western Hockey League's Kamloops Blazers probably came the closest of anyone. In a memorable run between 1992 and 1995, the British Columbia team won three of four Memorial Cups, symbolic of Canadian junior hockey supremacy.

"It started with our management group, one of the best in junior hockey, ever," said Darcy Tucker, a member of all three title teams and one of their many NHL graduates.

"You look at the team we had. Bob Brown, our general manager, seemed to find kids that not only had talent, but had good character. He found people who were willing to do whatever it took to win games and pay the price.

"Those players went on to the NHL and the young guys that came in learned from the veterans. That started

> **"The key against Kamloops was to get out of their building alive after the first ten minutes of the game."**
> – Tri-Cities Americans GM Dennis Beyak

with the group that won it for us the first year, that had [future big-league defensemen] Darryl Sydor and Scott Niedermayer. But a guy such as Zac Boyer scored with 14 seconds left to win the first title."

After a year's hiatus when coach Ted Nolan's Sault Ste. Marie Greyhounds brought the Memorial Cup to Ontario, the Blazers came back to win two straight, starting with Tucker's "sweetest" win, in Laval, Quebec.

"I'd been drafted by Montreal and to go in there and win in the backyard of the Canadiens was a thrill," Tucker said. "All the media coverage helped me as my career went on, in terms of dealing with pressure, media and other stressful situations.

"The third Cup was at home, with all our fans there. We'd won the WHL and it was just a dream season. We were ranked No. 1 from start to finish and we hosted it. It was one of those teams and one of those years where everything went right."

Darcy Tucker's intensity set the tone for his teammates. He twice led the Blazers in playoff scoring during their incredible run.

Stevie Y: A Red Wing for Life

The Motor City prides itself on producing quality sports vehicles, and Steve Yzerman has run smoothly year after year after year.

He completed 21 seasons with the Detroit Red Wings in the spring of 2004, cut short by a horrific facial injury when a puck struck just above his eye.

The year before, he'd undergone an osteotomy — a complicated realignment procedure on his right knee — a first for an active athlete. The specialist who operated, gave Yzerman a 50-50 chance of playing in the summer of 2002.

"I've never had it happen before," said coach Scotty Bowman at the time. "I've had players [stay out] with the same kind of knee problem. He just iced it and kept on playing. He got assurance that he can't do any more damage to it. It takes a lot of guts to do what he's doing, that's for sure."

Yzerman played in the 2002 Olympics and won a gold medal with Canada, then became one of just three NHLers ever to win a Stanley Cup the same year, joining teammate Brendan Shanahan and New York Islanders Ken Morrow. He sat out much of the Wings' final quarter of the 2001–02 schedule, but few complained when he helped deliver the club's third championship in six years.

> "A lot of things have to fall into place for a guy to stay in the same city for a long time. There were a couple of times when it was possible I might be traded."
>
> – Steve Yzerman

After 59 points in 91 games the past two seasons, can the longest-serving captain in NHL history come back for a full year at age 39?

"The way [Yzerman] plays, how hard he works, makes us all an inch taller," rival Eric Lindros said.

There were times he was ticketed out of town in contract disputes or when it seemed the Wings needed an overhaul. But Yzerman became synonymous with owner Mike Ilitch's complete revamping of the Wings in the early 1980s. Season tickets were down to about 2,000, and the Wings gave even their die-hard fans little reason to trip down to Joe Louis Arena.

Four clubs had a shot at Yzerman in the 1983 draft — the Wings, the Hartford Whalers, the Minnesota North Stars and the New York Islanders, in the midst of four consecutive Cups. Not surprisingly, Yzerman hoped for the Isles, but didn't balk when his ticket was punched for Detroit, home of Mr. Hockey, Gordie Howe.

"That's one of the special things about playing with a team that has a good history," Yzerman said. "And winning those championships? That's really helped me enjoy the whole experience."

The consummate captain, Yzerman's 155 points in 1988–89 are the most by any player not named Gretzky or Lemieux.

Star Power at its Best: The 1987 Canada Cup

The hockey stars might never again align as perfectly or brightly as they did in the late summer of 1987.

The game's greatest players from every hockey nation gathered for the Canada Cup, which came down to a best-of-three final between the host nation and Russia. This was the final international hurrah for the vaunted Red Machine, with Sergei Makarov, Vladimir Krutov and Slava Fetisov soon to leave for the NHL.

On the Canadian side, it was to be the last time Wayne Gretzky and Mario Lemieux — the dominant scorers of the 1980s at the height of their careers — would appear together.

"I'm excited and I think everyone in this dressing room is excited," Gretzky said the day before the classic series began at the Montreal Forum.

After moving ahead 4–1 early in the second period, Russia fell victim to a full-bore Canadian comeback, as elite players and grinders alike bit into the lead. Canada surged ahead 5–4, until a fluke goal hit Gretzky, goalie Grant Fuhr and defenseman Ray Bourque before sliding over the line. Then the visitors showed they, too, had a flair for the dramatic, winning in overtime on an Alexander Semak wrist shot.

> "I was going to No. 66 whether he wanted it or not."
>
> – Wayne Gretzky

The series shifted to Hamilton, Ontario, where the fans pulled out all the stops and covered Copps Coliseum with flags and banners. The excitement paid off in a goal just 43 seconds in, but just like Game 1, it was far from over.

It took overtime and more than four hours of hockey before Gretzky and Lemieux, banging away at the crease, evened the set in a 6–5 decision. Gretzky had five assists in the game.

The rubber match saw the Soviets take another commanding lead, 3–0, before the period was 10 minutes old. Coach Mike Keenan turned his tigers loose, namely Rick Tocchet, Brent Sutter and Mark Messier. Tocchet delivered a couple of big checks and scored to get the quiet fans back in the game. The only sure thing about the outcome in the concluding minutes was a third straight 6–5 result, the same score as Game 8 of the Summit Series 15 years earlier.

Keenan outmaneuvered the Russians to get Gretzky and Lemieux out against an inexperienced defense pair. A little skullduggery behind the play by Dale Hawerchuk created an odd-man rush. Using Larry Murphy as the decoy, Gretzky fed No. 66 for the winner with 1:26 to play in regulation.

"It was a fitting ending," Keenan said.

▌Wayne Gretzky called his performance in Game 3 of the final the greatest of his storied career.

The Invasion of the Sutters

From ball hockey battles in a hayloft to NHL immortality, the six Sutters remain the most remarkable brother act in pro sports.

From Brian's debut with the St. Louis Blues in 1976 through Ron's retirement with the Calgary Flames in 2001, at least one of the six-pack from Viking, Alberta, was active in the league.

They played a combined 4,994 games, with 2,935 points and 7,224 penalty minutes. Darryl and Brian remain active coaches in the NHL (Darryl guiding the Flames to the 2004 Cup finals), while the others are in scouting or related hockey businesses.

All six (the seventh and eldest brother, Gary, did not make the NHL) credit parents Louie and Grace for instilling the basic value of hard work for reward. The couple ran a livestock farm in tiny Viking, and the boys understood their chores were not to interfere with hockey.

"Dad would put all his money in seed and feed and things for the farm and then it wouldn't rain," Brian recalled. "I know it hurt him, hell, destroyed him inside, but he wouldn't let on. It's called being a man and dealing with problems."

"Sutter hockey" evolved from those highly charged games in the loft. When Louie would throw a bale of hay

> **"We never thought much about having six brothers in the NHL. First off, it was Brian's dream. When he made it, it became Darryl's and so on down the line."**
>
> – Brent Sutter

up there, his boys would throw it back down until their games ended. Grace had to try and milk cows through all the racket and sometimes simply hid her kids' tennis ball until cooler heads prevailed.

Brian arrived in the NHL first, one of the least naturally talented brothers, but with the heart of a lion. He later become captain of the Blues.

Duane and Darryl both broke in a few years later, then Brent joined Duane with the New York Islanders in time for four Stanley Cups. The two Isles were respectful enough of Brian and Darryl to never wear their Cup rings during summer reunions in Viking.

Twins Ron and Rich were picked by the Flyers and the Penguins in the early 1980s and eventually played together in Philadelphia. On October 30, 1983, Ron and Rich took on Brent and Duane for the first time, an event underscored by the Flyers–Isles rivalry at the time.

"Very few players have all the attributes, but the Sutters have them," sports psychologist Cal Botterill said in the book *Six Shooters*. "They're energized when other players are flat, loose when others are tight, confident when others are discouraged, respectful when others are overconfident, team people when others are bailing out and they keep their heads when others are overloaded."

Known for their grit and determination, the six Sutter brothers have made an invaluable contribution to the game of hockey.

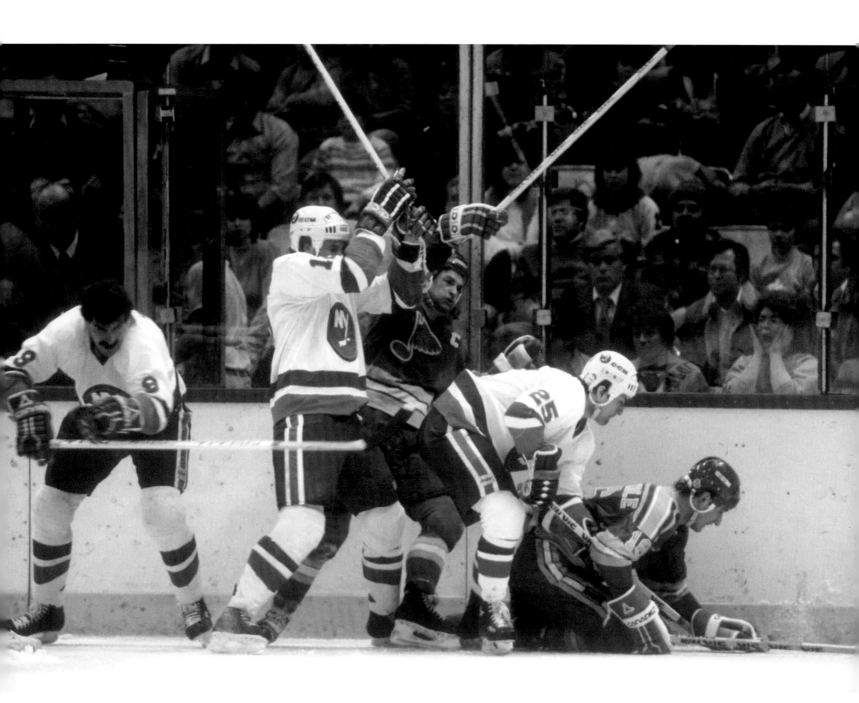

The Trials and Triumphs of Lucky Luc

His nickname was Lucky Luc, but you don't score 653 goals and lead all left wingers in NHL history by relying solely on good bounces.

Luc Robitaille was still banging in big goals from his close-range cottage after 18 seasons, completing 2003–04 as a top gun on the Los Angeles Kings with 22 goals and team-high 51 points. That was double his number of the previous season and gave him hope of breaking the 700 barrier before he turns 40 in 2006.

The Montreal native came into the league a very late draft choice, 171st overall in 1984. Despite getting 55 and 68 goals in Hull the two years after he was picked, some thought the sniper from the Olympiques would wilt once removed from the Quebec Major Junior Hockey League. Supposedly, he was too slow for the NHL.

But he won the Calder Trophy with 45 goals for the Kings in 1986–87, following it up with the first of three 50-goal seasons.

"I spent my first few years wanting to prove that I could play," he said. "But after a while, you start realizing that the reason you play is that you love the game and want to win championships."

That latter quest took far longer than expected. The Wayne Gretzky–era Kings came close to the Stanley Cup in 1993, but a dispirited Robitaille was traded a year later when they missed the playoffs. He went to Pittsburgh in a

> **"Players don't play for the chance at the Hall of Fame. They want to win the Cup."**
>
> – Luc Robitaille

year Mario Lemieux missed and then spent two years with the Rangers, who were suffering their own Cup hangover. Another three years with the Kings didn't see the club get past the second round.

It was then that he heard what was going on with the folks home in Detroit. Midway through that 2001–02 year with the Red Wings, he passed Bobby Hull for goals by a portside winger with 611. Hull was in the stands at Joe Louis Arena that night, the same game his son Brett moved ahead of him for third place in game-winning goals with 99.

"It's anticipation, a knowledge of the game, the ability to go to the right spot at the right time," Brett said of Robitaille. "Plus, he played on a lot of offensive teams in Los Angeles. Look at Mike Modano. If you set him free from that defensive system in Dallas, he'd have 500 goals by now."

The first pair of skates Robitaille owned were a Bobby Hull CCM model; Hull presented Robitaille with a cigar after the game. "I didn't know who to give it to, Brett or Luc," Hull said. "I'll just give Brett my love."

"It's going to be meaningful once I retire," Robitaille said of the record. "But I don't want to stop. I want to win a Cup."

That came true on June 13, 2002, when the Wings dispatched the Carolina Hurricanes in five games.

Winner of the 1987 Calder Trophy after scoring 45 goals as a rookie, Lucky Luc, an eight time All-Star, has secured his spot in the Hockey Hall of Fame.

Mess Takes Manhattan

They do things big in New York City, none bigger than Mark Messier's famous vow to keep the Rangers in the hunt for their first Stanley Cup in 54 years.

Down 3–2 to the New Jersey Devils in the Eastern Conference final, the ghosts of past failures were gathering around Madison Square Garden.

"It wasn't like you could avoid it," ex-Ranger Nick Kypreos said of the "curse." "It was everywhere; in the newspapers, on TV, from the fans. You'd be getting to the arena two hours before a game and 20 or 30 people would be at the gate to remind you. You couldn't buy pack a gum anywhere around MSG without someone mentioning it."

The Rangers began suspecting there was some kind of evil force at work as the Devils began to chip away at their veteran lineup and turn a 2–1 series lead into a 3–2 deficit. New York was a loss away from elimination.

"When Mark made his speech, he'd actually just said it to me and a couple of other people around him," winger Joey Kocur recalled. "It wasn't supposed to get out in the press, but when it did, it took on a life of its own."

With the surging Devils taking a 2–0 first-period lead,

> ## "We know we're going to go in and win Game 6 and bring it back for Game 7."
>
> – Mark Messier in the 1994 Eastern Conference final

all seemed lost. But an Alexei Kovalev goal set the stage for something that New Yorkers would later compare to Babe Ruth's called-shot home run.

Messier first put a backhand off a Kovalev pass behind Martin Brodeur, then tucked in a Kovalev rebound, before finishing with an empty-net goal.

"It was the kind of thing that leaders and superstars say," Kocur said. "He went out and got a hat trick."

The Rangers weren't out of the woods yet, having to win Game 7 and then rush back into action in the Cup final against Vancouver. After a surprising start by the Rangers, the Canucks gnawed away at the Rangers 3–1 series lead and forced a another cross-continent trip for a Game 7 at Madison Square Garden. The Rangers sweated out a 3–2 final. As the Cup at last went on its victory lap with Messier, a sign in the crowd said: "Now I Can Die in Peace."

"To this day, ten years after we won, people thank you for winning them a championship in their lifetime," Kypreos said. "For guys such as Mike Richter, Brian Leetch and Messier, who truly carried that Cup burden, winning was unbelievable, like a 5,000-pound weight had been lifted."

Messier scored the Cup-winning goal and became the only player to captain two different franchises to Stanley Cups. In doing so, he cemented his place as one of the greatest leaders in the history of sport.

Czech it Out:
A Gold-Medal Upset

Nagano, Japan, was supposed to be a National Hockey League showcase. Finally, after 70 years, the NHL's best would play in the light of the Olympic torch, particularly Canada and the U.S.

They should have heeded the warning from Czech Republic co-coach Slavomir Lener.

"Hockey experts in North America may not realize that many of the Czechs playing in Europe are as good or even better than those who play for NHL teams," he said.

As the tourney progressed, the mix of national program players and NHLers such as Dominik Hasek, Robert Reichel and Jaromir Jagr proved unshakable. David Moravec, a Czech League regular, came to prominence, as did a young Milan Hejduk, soon to take the NHL by storm in Colorado.

Hasek allowed one goal against the Americans in the quarter-final and then went into a 1–1 shootout duel with Patrick Roy in the semi's against Canada. He stoned Theoren Fleury, Ray Bourque, Joe Nieuwendyk, Eric Lindros and Brendan Shanahan. Wayne Gretzky was not picked by coach Marc Crawford.

Reichel had the winning shot for the Czechs, knowing

> "At that moment, we knew that we would not be defeated. I would have bet my life on it."
>
> – Robert Reichel

he rarely, if ever, beat Roy in a regular-season game. But a penalty shot was a different matter.

"I never miss," Reichel said. "It's maybe once in your life [to qualify for the final]. I don't want to miss the chance."

The Czechs gripped each others shoulders on the bench as the shooters took their turns.

When Hasek made the last save, it was bedlam, though a final against Russia was still to be played. Hasek came up big again, the forwards embraced a strong defensive game and Petr Svoboda scored the 1–0 winner in the third period.

Less than a day later, the Czechs were home in front of 70,000 delirious fans in the Old Town Square in Prague. They chanted "Hasek to the Castle," suggesting he should be made president. "It was the biggest party since the revolution in 1989," Hasek said.

"I had a dream. The whole [Czech] team had a big dream to bring back a gold medal. The Czechs weren't the best team going into the tournament, but we beat three of the best teams. Well, at least they used to be the best teams."

The Czech win at the '98 Olympics was followed by three straight World Championships and two World Junior titles, thrusting them to the top of the hockey world.

Goodbye, Gardens:
The Closing of the Carlton St. Cashbox

The pre-game music the night the Gardens closed covered seven decades of life inside and outside the Carlton St. Cashbox.

"In the Mood." "As Time Goes By." "At the Hop." "Don't Let the Sun Go Down on Me." "Glory Days." But when the horn sounded to end the last Gardens' Leafs game, it was the cue for many rounds of "Auld Lang Syne."

Called the most famous building in Canada, certainly the busiest from the 1960s through the 1980s, it had opened for hockey on November 12, 1931, and it closed February 13, 1999, bookended by losses to the Chicago Blackhawks.

But the memories in between were priceless pieces of Canadiana. The Leafs played 2,533 games at the Gardens, including playoffs, while their all-time regular season win-loss mark was 1,125–786–346. Eleven Stanley Cup banners were left hanging in its rafters when the Leafs moved.

"It was such an honest place to play hockey," Leafs player-coach-broadcaster Howie Meeker said. "I don't think they can build a building like this again."

People had been complaining for years about the Gardens being too old, too hot and too cramped, but in the end the 15,726 in attendance that final evening found it hard to say goodbye.

> **"Fans didn't live here like I did. But they did in their dreams."**
>
> – Maple Leaf Gardens P.A. announcer Paul Morris

Conn Smythe built the place to last, six stories at each corner, rising to 15 stories in the middle. It was constructed in an astounding five and half months in the early part of the Depression, with the financing made possible only when workers took part of their pay in Gardens stock. The materials included 750,000 bricks, 77,500 bags of cement, 70 tons of sand, 950,000 feet of lumber and 230,000 halite blocks.

On the final night, alumni going back to 1920s captain Red Horner were brought back. Horner gave a ceremonial Gardens flag to current captain Mats Sundin to be raised at the new Air Canada Centre.

"Mats, take this to our new home, but always remember us," Horner said as the chapter closed.

But the team also honored off-ice personalities that night, from ushers to 100-year-old former concession stand worker Bessie Lamson to the Zamboni driver. Also saluted was Paul Morris, whose father, Doug, was the building's first superintendent and a hockey innovator. Paul had a personal streak of 1,561 games as the Leafs' public address announcer, going back to October 1961.

"Bricks and mortar, you can get anywhere," ex-Leaf Tiger Williams said. "But it's the people that count. That's what I'll remember about the Gardens."

> "If the Gardens could talk, what a story it would tell. The Gardens is more than just bricks, concrete and steel. It's the people through the years who made it the mecca it became." – Brian Conacher

A Fistful of Title Rings for Canadian Juniors

For five unforgettable years, Canada had the Midas touch in junior hockey. Red, white and gold became the traditional Christmas tournament color from 1993 through 1997.

Five different coaches directed the team and shared in the glory: Perry Pearn, Joe Canale, Don Hay, Marcel Comeau and Mike Babcock. Chief scout Sheldon Ferguson was in charge for the first three wins and was credited for setting the program in motion.

Forward Jason Botterill played on three of the teams (1994, 1995 and 1996), in which the combined record was an incredible 30–3–1. That included an 18-game win streak that started midway through the 1994 tourney and continued until early in 1997. But each of the Canadian teams had a unique identity.

The 1993 squad's average age was 18.8, the youngest of the five. Chris Pronger, Chris Gratton, Alexandre Daigle, Paul Kariya and Rob Niedermayer had not even been drafted, but the big story was Manny Legace allowing only 10 goals in six games. It's considered the best netminding job of the five.

The no-name team of 1994 had to get by without 10 players who weren't released by NHL clubs or the Olympic program. But Todd Harvey, Jason Allison and Anson Carter used it as their coming-out party.

With the NHL locked out in 1995, a fortified Canadian dream team blasted its way to a perfect 7–0 record, the nation's first such sweep in WJC history.

More future NHL stars were on display in 1996, as Jose Theodore and Jarome Iginla helped lead the team to victory. Both went on to play in Canada a few years later, Theodore with Montreal, Iginla with Calgary. They were engaged in the tightest Hart Trophy vote ever, with Theodore squeaking out a win. Iginla won tourney MVP honors in 1996 with 12 points in six games.

The 1997 club was counted out after two losses early in the tournament. But unheralded stars such as Alyn McCauley, Boyd Devereux and goalie Marc Denis were the heroes in a 2–0 win over the Americans. McCauley, ailing with bronchitis, won several key face-offs, while Denis didn't allow a goal in the final 90:04.

Canada has not won the gold since, blowing a lead and losing to a determined Team USA squad in 2004.

> **"Our names will be etched in history. We got that fifth one."**
> – Team Canada forward Christian Dube at the 1997 World Junior Championships in Geneva

Canadian hockey fans were dealt a blow when the run of five straight championships came to an end. After not losing a game during the previous four tournaments, the Canadian squad lost five times at the '98 World Juniors in Finland.

Clever Devils Found New Ways to Win

Lou Lamoriello doesn't tolerate losing for very long. But where other teams make rash judgments in the name of improving, the New Jersey Devils tend to push the right buttons.

It's paid off in three Stanley Cups between 1995 and 2003 in an ultra-competitive NHL where most teams are lucky to get one. The Devils have drafted astutely, made key deadline trades and, in 2000, they fired coach Robbie Ftorek in the closing weeks of a first-place, 105-point season, replaced him with Larry Robinson and still won a Cup.

"I fill when empty, empty when full and scratch when it itches."

— New Jersey Devils president Lou Lamoriello

Lamoriello's teams, unlike the free spenders, are built from the ground up. As the 2003–04 season came to a close, the club retained 1990 No. 1 draft pick Martin Brodeur in goal, 1991's Scott Niedermayer and 2000's David Hale on defense and 1998's Scott Gomez up front. That's in addition to second rounders Patrik Elias, Jay Pandolfo, Colin White and Sergei Brylin and third rounders such as defenseman Paul Martin and forward Brian Gionta.

David Conte, the club's director of scouting, is often approached by teams that would like to make him a general manager.

The number of drafted Devils that the club traded for help or who otherwise departed is just as noteworthy, names such as Bill Guerin, Mike Dunham, Sheldon Souray, Brendan Morrison, Alyn McCauley, Mike Van Ryn, Brian Rolston and Stephane Yelle.

The Devils' most recent Cup saw them fight the surprising Mighty Ducks of Anaheim to the wire and win in a seventh game.

"Of the three, this year was probably the most difficult year of all," said defenseman Ken Daneyko, a first-round pick in 1982 who retired hoisting the Cup.

The 2003–04 season was one of upheaval for Lamoriello and the Devils. The club finished with 100 points, the eighth time in 11 seasons they've been in triple figures, but spiritual leader Scott Stevens missed the latter part of the year with post-concussion syndrome. The Devils didn't have home ice in the first round of the 2004 playoffs and lost to the Philadelphia Flyers.

After the series, coach Pat Burns was diagnosed with colon cancer. But he hopes to beat the disease and rejoin Lamoriello in putting the Devils back on the rails.

When Larry Robinson joined the Devils as an assistant coach, he brought with him a wealth of experience. They won their first Cup in franchise history in 1994–95.

A Game Blessed by St. Patrick

May 28 could be declared an NHL holiday, at least by those who don't wear goal pads. That was the date in 2003 that Patrick Roy bid the game adieu, with 702 regular season and playoff wins. He went out on top, after a 35-win season for the Colorado Avalanche and his second-lowest goals-against average of 2.18.

"It always has been important for me to play with consistency, but also to leave on my own terms," Roy said.

An appreciative crowd at the Pepsi Center in Denver gave him a four-minute standing ovation the following October, as his famous No. 33 went into the rafters with the two Stanley Cup banners he helped bring the city.

"I remember going to the rink for the first time with my parents and my brothers [in Quebec] when I was eight," Roy recalled. "To stand here in front of you tonight, 30 years later, is priceless."

One day, if the Montreal Canadiens change their minds about such ceremonies, Roy's number will also be in the Bell Centre, with the two Cups he earned as a Hab. It was in 1986 that Roy burst upon the scene there with a Conn Smythe Trophy performance. He dazzled with his butterfly stance, and chatted to his goal posts when he wasn't bantering with teammates or the press.

"Patrick is more than a goaltender," former coach Jacques Demers said. "He's one of the greatest athletes in Canada. The NHL is losing a great ambassador."

> **"I think I've accomplished everything I wanted. It's hard to imagine doing much more."**
>
> – Patrick Roy

When Roy retired, he held nearly every major goaltending record. He is the only three-time winner of the Conn Smythe, and is the league's career leader in wins and games, as well as wins, games and shutouts in playoffs. Hundreds of shooters would be haunted by the five-hole that Roy exposed as he dropped into the butterfly, but quickly closed like a fly trap. He bounced in and out of the stance with incredible ease and spawned a field of imitators in his home province, until hip problems slowed him down.

"It is our privilege that the Avalanche will retire the jersey of the greatest goalie to ever play," general manager Pierre Lacroix said at the sweater ceremony.

Roy could have stayed at least another year in the NHL, but opted not to take the final year of his contract with Colorado. He instead moved back to Quebec City to get involved with the local Remparts junior team.

Roy's spirit was probably best summed up with that famous wink through his mask after robbing Tomas Sandstrom of the Los Angeles Kings during the 1993 Cup final. He also had a temper, which boiled over on December 2, 1995, when Canadiens coach Mario Tremblay left him in for nine goals of an 11–1 loss to Detroit. Roy stormed past Tremblay and club ownership on the bench, demanding — and getting — a trade to the Avs.

In guiding the Avalanche to the 2000–01 Stanley Cup, Roy became the first player in NHL history to win the Conn Smythe Trophy as playoff MVP three times.

Everybody Loves Raymond

Ray Bourque had a multitude of awards, but always kept a place on his mantle open for a picture of him holding the Stanley Cup.

Five years turned into ten, which turned into 15 and then 20 for the career Boston Bruin. Until one of the greatest defensemen in NHL history hooked up with one of the top franchises of the post-expansion era, the Colorado Avalanche.

It wasn't long before all of Denver — and at least half of Massachusetts — got on the Mission 16 bandwagon. That was the hat Bourque and his teammates wore to count down the 16 wins to the Cup.

Bourque had come to the right place. Since moving from Quebec City in 1995–96, the Avalanche had won the Cup their first year, captured six straight Northwest Division titles, and never finished with less than 95 points.

The lineup, built in Quebec and refurbished after the move, included All-Stars Joe Sakic, Patrick Roy and Peter Forsberg. Avs general manager Pierre Lacroix immediately started a tradition of kickstarting the team with big trades. In 2000–01 that would include Bourque, though it was hard for him to leave Boston.

"In twenty-and-a-half years in Boston, with all the troubles pro athletes have been in, Ray was never a problem," said Kevin Paul Dupont, who covered Bourque

> **"That's why we made the move from Boston. My family knew why I was making it and now they are living [the dream]."**
>
> – Ray Bourque

for years with the *Boston Globe*. "He's a big story, no doubt. He's been ranked with Ted Williams and Carl Yastrzemski, the Boston guys who didn't win the big one."

With Bourque aboard, the Avs began chipping away at the Western Conference until they wound up in a seven-game Cup final with the defending champion New Jersey Devils. Bourque assisted on the winning goal in Game 3, and his wish came true a few nights later when the Avs won it all.

In the fastest handoff of the Cup by the winning captain, Sakic took it from commissioner Gary Bettman and thrust it at Bourque, who gave it the kiss he'd waited 22 years to plant.

"Lifting the Cup. . . what a feeling," Bourque said.

Bourque, not Sakic, then took the first long lap around the Pepsi Center. To the sounds of Louis Armstrong's "Wonderful World," Bourque held it high, while his wife, Christiane, and their three children wept.

Canadian Prime Minister Jean Chretien gave him a congratulatory phone call in the victor's dressing room, but Bourque didn't forget his five Norris Trophy years with the Bruins.

"I can't say enough about Boston," Bourque added. "I had two cracks at the Cup there. Everyone I played with there has a little piece of this."

Bourque retired a few weeks later.

Ray Bourque was chosen a league All-Star every year he was in the NHL and won the Norris Trophy as the league's best defenseman five times.

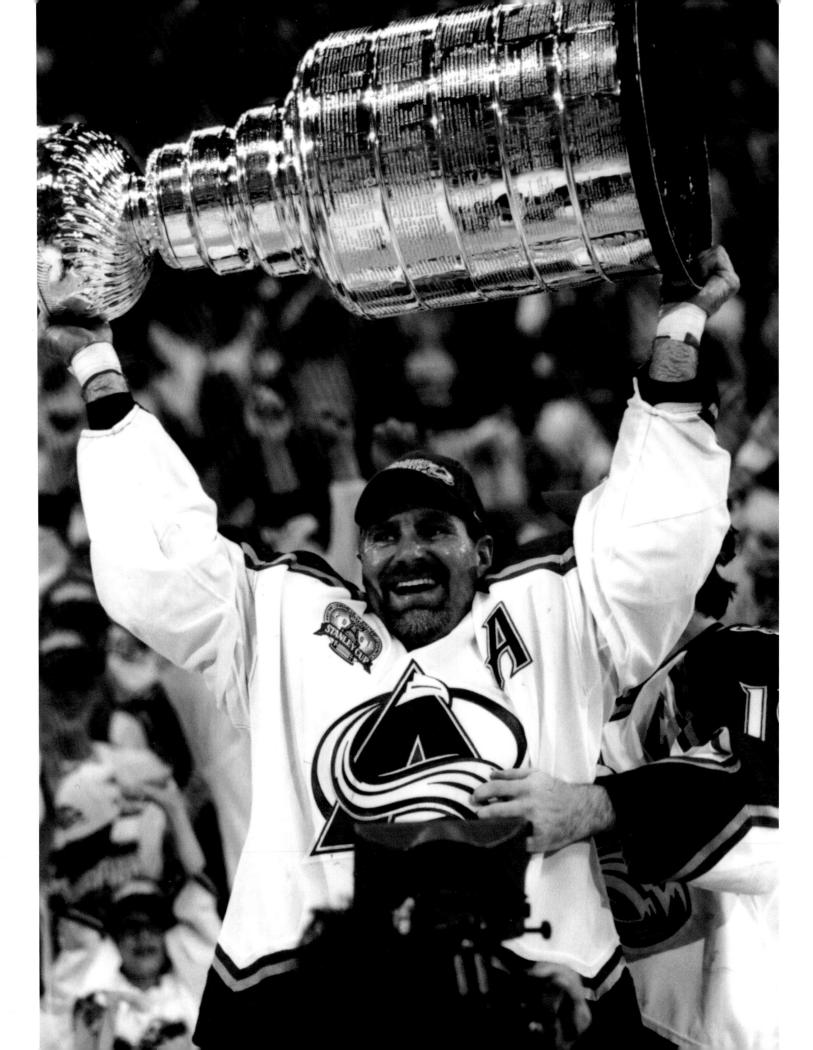

The End of an Era:
No. 99 Has Left the Building

All good things must come to an end, but the Great One will never be forgotten. On April 18, 1999, Wayne Gretzky played his last ever National Hockey League game, closing the most amazing individual chapter in the game's history.

Letting go was tough for Gretzky as he came out three times from the dressing room for curtain calls after his New York Rangers lost at home in overtime to the Pittsburgh Penguins. Gretzky ended with an assist on a Brian Leetch goal.

"It's going to kill me not to play."
– Wayne Gretzky

He collected the dozens of flowers and hats tossed his way, and when he finally submitted himself for his last press scrum as a player, he couldn't bring himself to strip off his famous No. 99 sweater.

"Probably subconsciously I didn't want to take it off," Gretzky said. "It's hard. I'll be honest. I don't want to take it off."

When he finally removed it, the jersey was immediately shipped to the Hall of Fame. Like his scoring records, the jersey will be seen and not touched.

In 1,487 games spanning 20 seasons, he had 894 goals and 1,963 assists for 2,857 points. Add to that last number 382 playoff points in pursuit of four Stanley Cups with the Edmonton Oilers. In all, he left the game holding more than 60 scoring records.

His minor hockey, junior, World Hockey Association and national team numbers were also stunning when seen in the light of his retirement.

"But time does something to you and it's time," he said, after a center-ice hug with Mark Messier. "I feel really confident about my decision. [During a final Rangers timeout], I looked up and I said, 'My goodness, I've got 30 seconds to go.' That's when it hit me."

Gretzky spoke to Michael Jordan before the game and got to Madison Square Gardens in plenty of time to sign 51 sticks that would go to teammates and trainers as souvenirs of the game. Gordie Howe gave him a video tribute during the game.

Though Gretzky was almost swayed several times to change his mind by family and friends, his neck was very sore from the years of wear and tear, and the Rangers were his preferred final destination. He didn't want to be accused of hanging around with diminished talent just to cash in on his name.

So 1999 was the end for 99, and a fitting exit it was.

Quite simply the greatest player to ever play the game, Gretzky took everything in stride. Upon retirement, he reflected, "Dreams do come true, I'm living proof of that."

Bryan Berard Comes Back from an Eye Injury

In the wake of the horrific accident that all but blinded Bryan Berard's right eye, many writers called it a career-ending injury.

But Berard would defy the odds and come back 18 months later, determined not to give up his NHL dream. The Maple Leafs defenseman underwent seven operations after March 11, 2000, when Ottawa Senator Marian Hossa struck him on the follow-through of his shot.

Berard was fitted with a contact lens implant that brought him to minimum vision requirements for the league, though he realized that coming back in any capacity meant his days of initiating the rush and wide open hockey would have to be curtailed.

General manager Pat Quinn and the Leafs shepherded him through the months after the injury, but Berard thought it best to make a fresh start with another team.

He began the 2001–02 season with the New York Rangers, making slow progress, but adjusting to the hand fate had dealt him. By the end of the 2003–04 season, he had 47 points in 58 games for the Chicago Blackhawks, was top five on the team and was among the leading blue-liners in the league. He was awarded the Bill Masterton

> **"It might be the best comeback story of all time."**
>
> – Pat Quinn

Trophy that year for perseverance and dedication to hockey.

"It took me about a year to re-learn how to play with the good eye, but now, I really don't notice it," Berard said. "I don't think I'm anything special, I just go out on the ice and play.

"I don't want to just go out there and say I played again. I want to go out and be the best."

Surprisingly, Berard remained opposed to the introduction of mandatory face protection, even though a spate of eye injuries occured around the NHL and the minors in the years immediately after his mishap.

"We all have a choice and we all have that right," said Berard. "Sure, a visor probably would have saved me from what I went through, but each player should make that decision for themselves. Wearing one after was difficult at first for me but I pretty much have to wear one [for medical reasons]."

Berard didn't want people to dwell on the handicap, and neither did his coaches. "He has two eyes, just like the rest of us have," Boston Bruin Robbie Ftorek said during Berard's stop there in 2002–03. "It's what you do with what you have."

The winner of the 1996–97 Calder Trophy as rookie of the year, Berard (No. 34) has managed to return to form following his devastating injury. In 2004, he won the Bill Masterton Trophy, awarded for perseverance and dedication to hockey.

Gretzky Speech as Good as Gold

Wayne Gretzky is not known for losing his cool. But the 2002 Winter Olympics proved quite the stage for the game's greatest player to get a few things off of his chest as general manager of Team Canada.

Facing a 50-year drought of Olympic hockey gold, and losses in the 1996 World Cup and 1998 Olympics, Gretzky got the attention of his team and everyone else in Salt Lake City with a rant similar to the popular "I Am Canadian" beer ads.

Whether his comments were calculated or an honest reaction to rough stuff after a 3–3 tie with the Czech Republic, they certainly put Canada on high alert in the medal-round games.

While gold-medal hopefuls Sweden and Russia were knocked off along the way, Canada and the United States fashioned records of 3–1–1 and made it to the championship game. Part of Canada's problem in 1998 was not being able to find the right balance of scorers and checkers, but in 2002 a new staff under Gretzky and head coach Pat Quinn took the most talented players, period, and asked them to tailor their games and do the necessary dirty work.

> **"I know the whole world wants us to lose, except Canada and Canadian fans and our players."**
> – Wayne Gretzky

"We said we'll take the most talented guys, the guys that can skate, the guys that can think, and we'll ask them to play the game both ways," Quinn said. "And they can, usually as well or better than the grinders."

The results were impressive as the tourney went on. By the final, Canada had allowed just 12 goals in five games.

A Tony Amonte goal put the Americans in front for the gold, an unsettling situation, given that Canada had scored first throughout the tournament. But Canada tied it up in spectacular fashion, with Mario Lemieux letting a Chris Pronger pass drift through his legs for Paul Kariya to drive in, an artistic, soccer-style goal.

The stars on both teams put on quite a show, despite the high altitude in Utah that made it tough to recover from long shifts.

"I've had people come up to me who've never watched a game of hockey in their lives, but watched the Olympics and said, 'This is the greatest stuff I've ever seen,'" Kariya said.

Joe Sakic had two goals and an assist in the game, and Martin Brodeur was sharp in goal as Canada prevailed.

After a series of disappointing results on the world stage, Canadian hockey found itself on top again after the inspired performance in Salt Lake City.

Women Wear Gold

The world isn't very big when you play for the Canadian or U.S. national women's hockey teams. The two nations have met in the final of all eight International Ice Hockey Federation championships and in the past two Olympic gold-medal games.

While some games in the early stages of these tournaments turn into double-digit blowouts, the title game rarely disappoints when the two hockey powers clash.

That was the case again in Halifax, Nova Scotia, in the spring of 2004. Team Canada hung on for a 2–0 win, after its streak of 37 straight triumphs in the tournament was halted by the U.S. in the preliminary round. It was Canada's eighth win at the world championships, while the two teams split the Olympic title in 1998 and 2002. Hayley Wickenheiser's goal in Halifax stood up as the game-winner.

"We did some (good) things today that we haven't done for years," said Wickenheiser, who began the 2003–04 season playing against men in the Finnish League. "This event gets better and better every year. It's an exciting product to watch."

> "I don't know too many teams in this country that have won eight championships in a row. This team comes through when it has to."
>
> – Team Canada forward Hayley Wickenheiser

Young female players in both nations who have yearned for something to shoot for after minor hockey, were no doubt inspired by what they saw in the final. As usual, the two countries held nothing back. Opposing goalies Kim St.-Pierre of Canada and Pam Dreyer of the U.S. turned aside a number of quality chances. American Natalie Darwitz scored to make it 2–1 with five minutes to play, but game officials had no access to a TV feed, which showed the puck quickly going in and out under the crossbar.

The IIHF does not yet have an established video replay system in place at the women's level. At the 2004 men's championship, Canada won in overtime when video backed up Anson Carter's gold-medal goal against Sweden.

But veteran American player Cammy Granato didn't dwell on sour grapes.

"This is my eighth championship and I've seen (Canada) win every time when it's on the line," Granato said.

After a devastating defeat to the Americans at the 1998 Olympic Games in Nagano, the Canadian women rejoiced upon claiming gold in Salt Lake City.

Scandinavian Suspense

For five minutes in the spring of 2003, the Vladimir Sindler Show was the most-watched in Canada, more compelling than *Survivor*, *The Bachelor* and *Friends* put together.

It's not every day the fate of the world — okay, the world hockey championships — is in the hands of a Czech referee and a Finnish TV technician.

Sindler was trying to figure out if Team Canada's Anson Carter had scored a legitimate goal on Swedish goaltender Mikael Tellqvist at 13:49 of overtime at the World Championships. Carter celebrated his wraparound shot as if the 3–2 win was a done deal, but Sindler called time and went to the video booth for confirmation.

The crowd at Helsinki's Hartwall Arena, the undefeated Canadians, the hungry Swedes and an international audience all held their breath. If it was ruled inconclusive, Carter was not sure he could play any more, as he'd twisted his knee in the initial goal celebration.

Finally, after looking at seven different camera angles, a welcome technological circumstance for Carter, Sindler put down the phone and pointed to center ice. The Canadians on the bench went wild the country's first world championship gold in five years.

> "I saw it go in. There was no doubt in my mind."
>
> – Anson Carter

In the Toronto suburb of Scarborough, Valma Carter wasn't all that surprised that her son had been the hero.

"Anson asked me what I wanted for Mother's Day [that weekend] and I said 'nothing but that gold medal, and you'd better deliver,'" she said. "And he delivered."

Carter shared the glory with goaltender Roberto Luongo. After giving up two goals early in the game, Luongo stopped Swedish star and Maple Leafs captain Mats Sundin twice on breakaways as part of 37 saves. Four years earlier on the international stage, Luongo had given up an overtime goal to Russia in the final of the world junior tournament.

"Now I know how it feels to be on the other side," Luongo said. "It's a beautiful day for Canada."

For players such as Carter, Luongo, Daniel Briere (nine points and two game-winning goals) and many others on Team Canada, gold was the ultimate consolation prize for not making the Stanley Cup playoffs.

Many of the same players were in Prague the next year, when Canada beat Sweden for the gold again, though in a less dramatic fashion.

Carter and his teammates returned home to a hero's welcome. Once merely a blip on the Canadian radar, the World Hockey Championships have become a venue for young Canadian stars to showcase their skills.

Little Big Man Wins His Biggest Battle

As one of the smallest players in the NHL, yet one who never shirks from bigger players, Saku Koivu knows courage.

But nothing could prepare the 27-year-old for what he would endure in the 2001–02 season, when he was diagnosed with non-Hodgkin's lymphoma just before the Canadiens training camp began. It was the same type of cancer that Mario Lemieux had recovered from a few years earlier, but there were more complications in Koivu's case and some doubt that he would live to see Christmas that year.

> **"We hung his sweater in the dressing room and we never forgot No. 11. We've been waiting for this all season."**
> – Canadiens defenseman Karl Dykhuis

Between the aggressive chemotherapy treatments, a gaunt-looking Koivu held a news conference to thank people in North America and his native Finland who had sent 30,000 e-mails, plus cards, flowers and letters. He mailed out 20,000 thank-you cards himself.

Not only did he survive, he was able to come back from several cycles of the chemotherapy the night his Montreal Canadiens clinched a playoff berth against the Ottawa Senators. A sellout home crowd of 21,273 chanted his name before he skated out, and gave him a standing ovation as he lined up for the national anthem.

"I never felt anything like that in my life," Koivu said. "The emotion from the fans was incredible. I expected something, but not that much. It shows the kind of fans we have here."

Koivu played 13 shifts in his return and was able to switch to the wing, an unfamiliar position.

"I would think this would be pretty emotional for the people of Montreal," Ottawa coach Jacques Martin said.

"We're talking about a guy who has had to battle for his life. That's a much bigger victory than tonight and it's quite an accomplishment."

Underweight from the disease and his chemo, Koivu played two more regular-season games and had 10 points in 12 playoff games as the Habs went two rounds that year. He had plenty of consultation with Chris Carmichael, the personal trainer who had helped multi–Tour de France winner Lance Armstrong get back in shape for the rigors of long-distance cycling.

"I can't believe the energy he has got," Lemieux said, after the two clashed in a game. "It's great to see him play again."

An inspiration to all, Koivu returned to the ice after six months away from the game. Exhausted and underweight from chemotherapy, he none the less tied for the team lead in playoff scoring.

Brian Boucher's Traveling Shutout Show

Not for a half-century had the NHL seen anything like Brian Boucher's traveling shutout show. What began with a 4–0 blanking of the Los Angeles Kings on New Year's Eve, 2003, at home in Phoenix, stretched to a modern-day-record five shutouts for the little-known goalie from Woonsocket, Rhode Island. (Because the NHL's modern era began with the 1943–44 season, Alex Connell is credited with the overall record of six shutouts in a row and a 461:29 scoreless streak for the Ottawa Senators in 1927–28.)

His mask designed with a brick–wall motif, Boucher recorded road shutouts in Dallas (on his 27th birthday), Carolina, Washington and Minnesota. In the last of these games, he broke the 1949 record of Montreal's Bill Durnan of 309 minutes, 21 seconds without a goal. (Durnan was quite a story on his own: an ambidextrous goalie who played baseball in the off-season and played net with two crude gloves resembling neither catcher nor blocker.)

"The puck doesn't look bigger, but I'm seeing it real well right now," Boucher said after his fifth shutout. "But you've got to be prepared that it's going to end."

It ended in the next game at home against the Atlanta Thrashers. At 6:16 of the first period, Randy Robitaille's power-play shot struck Coyotes' defenseman David Tanabe in the chest and went in. Boucher had made 146 consecutive saves prior to that fluke and kept the puck out an astounding five-and-a-half hours of game time. Not bad for someone who was the Coyotes' third-string goaltender at the start of the season.

"I'm happy that it's over," Boucher said of the streak after the 1–1 tie. "It was a nice run, something I'll never forget. But I think it's good for the team that we don't have to answer questions about it anymore. A fluke. That's how easily a goal can go in. The fact that it didn't happen for five-plus games is pretty amazing."

Those five shutouts were the only ones Boucher had all year and represented half his wins. The Coyotes didn't make the playoffs.

> **"Sometimes bounces go your way. But at some point you have to say he's unbelievable."**
>
> – Phoenix captain Shane Doan

After bursting onto the scene with the Philadelphia Flyers in 1999–2000, Boucher has struggled to find his place in the NHL. Including his five consecutive shutouts, he managed to win only 10 games in the 2003–04 season, compared to 19 losses.

Hasek Dominated the Goal Lines and the Headlines

As one wry observer noted, he had a slinky for a spine, but Dominik Hasek also had a knack for getting in the news.

From the year he first won the Hart Trophy in 1996–97 to his aborted comeback in 2003–04, Hasek was never far from the top of the goaltending stats and was frequent front-page fodder for hockey columnists.

He was implicated in the implosion of the Cup-contending Buffalo Sabres in the late 1990s, roughed up a writer, retired on more than one occasion, was head-hunted by a Sabres teammate, was investigated in the Czech Republic for assaulting an in-line hockey player and was in constant peril of groin injuries.

But he's the same man who won new respect for goaltenders by getting a stopper's name restored to the Hart Trophy, not once but twice, leading the Czechs to an improbable gold medal in 1998 and winning a Stanley Cup for Detroit in 2002. "He's a human being sometimes misunderstood by the public," former Sabres chairman John Rigas said.

By his own admission, Hasek is a freak of goaltending nature, developing a floppy style, body splayed outward with his pads somehow able to stop low and high shots behind him.

"Nobody taught me how to play hockey," Hasek said. "They just told me to keep my stick on the ice and stop the puck. I tell the kids to watch all the goalies. I don't want to say my style is the best, but my style is the best for me."

He was almost squeezed out of the NHL when his first coach, Mike Keenan, chose Ed Belfour as the No. 1 goalie in Chicago. But as a Sabre, Hasek won 234 games and put the team back on the map. His behavior sometimes gets him in trouble, but it is partly balanced by his devoted charity work, including projects for disadvantaged youngsters.

Unrest in Buffalo eventually led to a trade to Detroit, where he won a career-best 41 games in 2001–02 and the Cup. He and coach Scotty Bowman retired within a few days of each other, and with a significant Cup bonus, Hasek seemed ready for the good life in the Czech Republic with his family.

But at 39, he came back to the Wings, creating a sticky situation with incumbents Curtis Joseph and Manny Legace. Another groin injury sidelined Hasek, simplifying the issue. Hasek will play for Ottawa in 2004–2005.

> **"The attention I receive is overwhelming. I don't enjoy it. I don't want to live behind a wall. I hope once I retire, it will be over."**
>
> – Dominik Hasek

Despite his unorthodox style and personality, Dominik Hasek must be considered one of the best goaltenders of all time. Twice awarded the Hart Trophy as league MVP and a six-time winner of the Vezina Trophy for top goalie, he backstopped the Red Wings to a Stanley Cup in 2002.

The Stars Came Out to Play Under the Stars

Hockey outdoors — what a concept! It took the NHL about 90 years to try it again, but the experiment on November 22, 2003, turned out to be the feel-good story of a season plagued by clouds of labor unrest and black eyes on the sport.

The Heritage Classic, a double-header of present and former Montreal Canadiens and Edmonton Oilers, was played on a clear day before 57,167 people at Commonwealth Stadium, at temperatures between –17° and –19° Celsius.

But the cold was part of the allure of seeing Wayne Gretzky back in Edmonton, in his first old-timer's match with Mark Messier and their Oiler buddies. The alumni opposition was the cream of Les Glorieux from the 1970s and 1980s, led by the magical Guy Lafleur.

"Our problem wasn't in getting enough guys, it was in deciding which guys to bring," Habs alumni director Rejean Houle said. "We could easily have brought 60." The Habs old-timers lost 2–0.

The nightcap was an official NHL regular-season game, which Montreal won 4–3. Slumping Hab Yanic Perreault dug out a pair of old Daoust skates from his basement for the game and scored twice.

The Habs old-timers wore tuques in the first game that were such a hit with goalie Jose Theodore and the current crew that they were washed, dried and loaned to the youngsters in time for the second game.

> "We really felt like we were ten-year-olds out there – with 50-year-old legs."
>
> – Guy Lafleur

"I thought that after the first game, when they saw Wayne (Gretzky), everybody was going to go home because it was so cold out there," Oiler Georges Laraque said.

"At the bench we had warmers, but the fans didn't. But they stayed for both games. You looked around and the stands were packed."

Alumni on both teams came from both sides of the Atlantic, while ticket requests, which early projections said might not fill half the football stadium, numbered around 900,000.

Gretzky's participation was up in the air until Oilers GM Kevin Lowe talked him into it. Once Gretzky warmed to the idea, he phoned Lafleur to bring the Habs, as the choice of a second team had not been determined. Other candidates had included the New York Rangers and the Calgary Flames.

"I'd never have forgave myself for not coming," said Messier, who was given permission to play the first game by Oilers-turned-Rangers GM Glen Sather.

There was a fly-by of Canadian fighter jets before the game, surely a hockey first. Gretzky's daughter Paulina sang between the two matches.

"It was a great experience, it was a great crowd," Oiler Jason Chimera said. "The weather wasn't a factor, we weren't cold. It was one of those things you remember for your whole life."

> The highlight of the 2003–04 season, the Heritage Classic allowed both players and fans to turn back the clock. Despite the cold temperatures, the game was a resounding success and will likely lead to more outdoor games for the NHL.

St. Louis at the Height of Greatness

They've debated his height for years, but there's no arguing his talents. Martin St. Louis, all five-foot-eight, 185 pounds of him, was the NHL's best player in 2003–04, just when people thought you needed a size XXL sweater to fulfill any major-league hockey dream.

St. Louis won the Art Ross Trophy for most points, with 94, helped his Tampa Bay Lightning to their first Stanley Cup, won the Lester B. Pearson Trophy (the players' choice for MVP) and the Hart Trophy (hockey writer's choice for MVP), and was a first team All-Star right winger.

"He puts people in the seats, people who want to see what he can do next," said Colorado Avalanche forward Joe Sakic.

St. Louis was listed as five-foot-nine through his first few NHL seasons, but on awards night, he finally admitted he was an inch shorter. The last Art Ross Trophy winner who was this vertically challenged was the five-foot-nine Stan Mikita back in 1968. Like Mikita, St. Louis adjusted to severe physical punishment, right through the Cup final against the rough-and-tumble Calgary Flames.

"It comes with the territory," St. Louis said. "I am aware of that. But what are you going to do? You can [complain to] the referees, but it is not going to help."

> "I do things a six-foot-three player can't do and there are things I can't do that a six-foot-three player can. Everybody finds a way to do things their own way."
>
> – Martin St. Louis

St. Louis's height has been held against him since he first tied on skates. He wasn't deemed ready to play major junior hockey, but joined a neighborhood amateur club in Laval, Quebec, and had a 103-point year. When he started setting scoring records after four seasons with the University of Vermont, the Calgary Flames signed him as a free agent. But they had him slotted as a fourth liner and eventually waived him away to Tampa Bay in 2000.

He not only beat out established stars such as Sakic and Vancouver's Markus Naslund for leading scorer, he and Ottawa's Daniel Alfredsson had the fewest penalty minutes (24) of anyone with 80 or more points.

"When you see yourself at the top, ahead of some big names, it is overwhelming," St. Louis said. "At the same time, you have to feel like you belong there, because if you don't, you won't be there long."

Teammates marvel at his courage under fire and his willingness to go to the net where many angels fear to tread.

"Martin scores his goals from everywhere," teammate Fredrik Modin said. "He has a good enough shot to score from a distance. He scores off the rush. He scores from the slot, from the crease, from everywhere."

St. Louis had a dream season in 2003–04. Aside from winning the Stanley Cup, he also won the Art Ross Trophy as the league's leading scorer, the Hart Trophy as league MVP and the Lester B. Pearson Award for MVP, as voted by his peers.

Lightning, Flames Caught in Cup Storm

Could Cinderella be in two places at once? In the 2004 Stanley Cup playoffs, it took two months, a grueling seven-game final and a one-goal decision on the last night to determine that there's room for just one fairytale ending per year.

The Calgary Flames, at times last year not even considered the best team in their province, beat three division winners and carried the hopes of Cup-deprived Canada into the June final. They came up just short in a 2–1 loss.

"When we look back, it will be memorable, but we could've made it more memorable," Flames forward Craig Conroy lamented.

But beating the upstart Flames hardly demonized the Tampa Bay Lightning, a team that had more Canadian-born players in its ranks than Calgary (12 to 10) and whose skill-oriented game proved just a bit more persuasive than the Flames' physical bent. Viewed as talented underachievers, the Lightning brought the Cup to the sunny climes of Florida for the first time, having won just one playoff series in their 11-year existence.

It was the most intense championship round in years, paying homage to 111 years of Cup lore. After each team won overtime games in the other's rink, Game 7 saw Vinny Lecavalier engineer one of the best Cup-winning goals ever, though a late-game, last-gasp charge by the Flames almost forced an extra period for all the marbles.

"You couldn't have written a better story," Lightning forward Martin St. Louis said.

The Flames had the inspiring efforts of captain Jarome Iginla, the clutch goals of Martin Gelinas, and Miikka Kiprusoff's cool hand in net. But Tampa was on a mission to end their captain Dave Andreychuk's 22-year Cup drought and fast-track a Cup plan that saw Lecavalier, Brad Richards and St. Louis all come of age.

In Calgary, where the area around the Pengrowth Saddledome had been designated the Red Mile for its raucous post-victory parties, the Flames struck a blow for small-market teams and served notice they're back on an even footing with the five other Canadian franchises. From April 7 to June 7, nine Flames were either knocked out of the playoffs with severe injuries or soldiered on with significant damage.

But Lightning stars such as St. Louis and Lecavalier came back from vicious hits in the series to prove their mettle, while Richards won the Conn Smythe Trophy.

"We were so close to a dream — to believe it could be us out there, holding the Cup," Iginla said. "I pray we get another chance."

> **"I've never been through something so draining in my life."**
> – Lightning coach John Tortorella

Jarome Iginla did everything he could to help his team throughout the playoffs. After the Flames defeated the Vancouver Canucks in Game 7 of their opening-round series, Canucks coach Mark Crawford stated that Iginla's performance that night was the most dominating he had ever seen in all his years in hockey.

Souvenirs

The Battered Old Mug That Could Tell Many a Tale

If what happens on the road to the Stanley Cup is the stuff of legend, consider what's happened to Stanley when it's on the road.

In days of yore, it was drop-kicked into the frozen Rideau Canal, used as a flower pot, and abandoned by the Canadiens on the side of the road when they stopped to fix a flat tire. Through ensuing years, teams have swigged beer, champagne and even dog food from its famous bowl.

But hockey players being the revelers they are, the hijinks don't stop there. The "People's Trophy" has also made visits to strip clubs and the bottom of Mario Lemieux's pool, and has been knocked around in just about every way imaginable.

While "Sparky" Kulchisky was known as the Keeper of the Cup in Edmonton, and more than once rescued it from crazy stunts at the hands of the five-time champions, the 1994 Rangers were not so careful.

After winning the Cup for the first time in 54 years, they brought it to such Big Apple locales as Yankee Stadium and the David Letterman studio, but got carried away at some point in the proceedings. The Cup they gave back to the league for display at the draft in Hartford that year was cracked at the top and almost severed, and had several dents.

> **"One morning, the boys brought Stanley in after a real hard run the night before. It was in two pieces. So I took it to the Freedom Ford body shop. They fixed Stanley good as new, just in time for a team function."**
>
> – Edmonton Oilers trainer Lyle Kulchisky

"It looks like someone sat on it," an upset Hockey Hall of Fame official said. But repairs were quickly made, and the tradition of each man getting a day with the century-old trophy was continued.

It wasn't just players who mishandled the mug. Two attempts were made to steal it from the Hall, one as a college prank. One was successful, though the thieves returned it when they found they'd stolen the substitute Cup by mistake.

In the late 1990s, the Cup began making trips to Japan and Europe and even took a ride on a dogsled prior to the 2004 All-Star game in Minnesota.

But one of its most fateful trips was in 1996 to Wilberforce, Ontario, where then-Colorado Avalanche Mike Ricci had brought it to his cottage. Ken and Cheryl Riley had only a loose connection to Ricci through Ken's boss, but the couple was driven by Cup curiosity to drop by.

Cheryl, who had been trying to have children for 17 years and had been told it was medically impossible, impulsively kissed the Cup. Lo and behold, in a couple of days she was pregnant, at age 42.

Stanley C. Riley was born in 1997.

The Stanley Cup is widely considered the hardest trophy in all of sport to win. This might explain the celebration that seems to follow it from town to town.

A Star is Born:
Hockey Enters the TV Age

When the red "On Air" light goes on and the *Hockey Night in Canada* theme strikes up, the faithful gather in front of the TV altar for the Church of Saturday Night.

In 2004, the Toronto Maple Leafs and Ottawa Senators played a Game 6 in front of almost four million viewers, the best ratings for a first-round game in a decade.

When the first black-and-white images of a televised hockey game were seen in the spring of 1952, it was a game with two junior teams, the Guelph Biltmores and the Regina Pats, and the audience was a small cluster of advertising executives watching on closed circuit.

The game was an experiment, a Memorial Cup match at Maple Leaf Gardens, and many fundamental arguments had to be thrashed out before an NHL broadcast could be incorporated. For one, Gardens patriarch Conn Smythe was leery of the new technology and didn't want cameras blocking the paying patrons.

That led to experiments with cameras in the far-off grey seats ("Might as well be watching the game in the suburbs," one exec complained) and the placement of a camera in Foster Hewitt's Gondola so that the audience could get the same vantage as the legendary broadcaster.

> "It's classic Canadian theatre, hockey and fantasy together."
> – former *Hockey Night in Canada* producer John Shannon

Smythe eventually agreed to a camera lower in the prime seats, but only if a matching one were placed directly across the rink. That was eventually dismissed as being too disorienting for the viewer.

But the ad men generally liked what they saw that day at the Gardens, and also what they heard. There was concern that the excitable Hewitt wouldn't be as appealing on TV as on radio, but many electrifying broadcasts later, this was proven otherwise.

Plans were made to put the Leafs on TV for the first time on November 1, 1952. But in Montreal, where there was no haggling about camera placement or broadcast styles, the Canadiens were able to help the Canadian Broadcasting Corporation get a telecast together for October 11, beating the Leafs.

Today, a typical hockey game takes a small army of technicians and talent to produce. New arenas build broadcast-friendly facilities with multiple camera angles, including one in the net. A glowing puck for American viewers to follow was experimented with and rejected in the 1990s.

Prominent teams have all their games televised, and the Leafs launched their own digital channel prior to the 2002–03 season.

Hockey Night in Canada has become a Canadian institution. When contract negotiations between the CBC and *Hockey Night* host Ron MacLean broke down, the CBC was flooded with calls insisting they take MacLean back. They did.

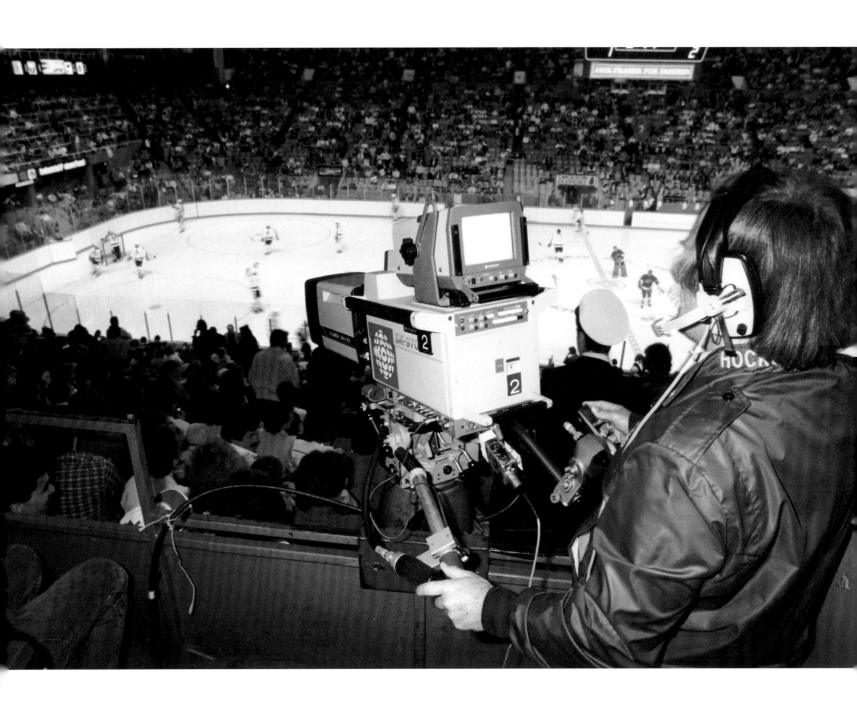

No Worlds Left to Conquer, Bowman Bows Out on Top

On June 13, 2002, with the Joe Louis Arena crowd in Cup celebration mode, Scotty Bowman walked off the Detroit Red Wings bench and into history.

"That was my last game," the most successful coach in pro hockey told goaltender Dominik Hasek as his 10th Cup-winning team took a victory lap after beating the Carolina Hurricanes 3–1. He then informed his wife, Suella, on his way to the podium for the official announcement.

What other way for Bowman to exit but on top? He had 1,244 overall wins, five Cups with the Montreal Canadiens, including their 1976–79 dynasty, two more with the Pittsburgh Penguins as both coach and player personnel boss, then the hat trick with Detroit. The nine Cups as coach put him ahead of Toe Blake, the man he idolized in Montreal when Bowman was getting his feet wet with the Junior Canadiens.

And though the 2002 Wings might not have been the best team he'd had, their relatively smooth ride to their third Cup in six years mirrored what kind of coach a more mellow Bowman had become.

In his first days with the expansion St. Louis Blues, he greeted the 40-man training camp by declaring, "None of you deserves to be here. If the league hadn't expanded, you'd all still be in the minors where you belong. So the 20 of you that make the team will be the ones who work hardest. Let's get at it."

> **"When you think of it, [Bowman] has spent most of his career being a tyrant. It's just that he became a lot more subtle about it in his later days."**
>
> – hockey columnist Al Strachan

In Montreal, he had such disdain for his media critics that he had them board the rickety short-haul charter plane first as ballast for the equipment in the back. He'd been told putting the gear in first might drop the plane's tail during fueling and cause a spark, thus he preferred to risk the media in case of mishap.

In his early days in Detroit, his players were virtually cut off from the press, while he delighted in such schemes as shortening the visitors' bench or painting their dressing room on game day, making them ill inhaling fumes.

But most of the time his sharp mind was focused on the ice. Matching wits with Bowman was a test for any of the young turks in the coaching ranks, and he was as good for the game's image as any star player.

Rivals such as the Leafs' Pat Quinn are amazed that he was able to get the most out of his teams through years of dramatic shifts in coach–player relationships. Hurricanes coach Paul Maurice, beaten in the 2002 final, took solace in knowing he'd lost to the best in the business.

"In a 30-team league, no one is going to come close to this guy," Maurice said.

Bowman was quick to respect those players he deemed worthy of it. He said of Steve Yzerman, "He's one of those players, and there are few, who come to work every day."

Willie Blazed a Trail on the Ice

In an age when hockey fans welcome six or seven different nationalities on a team's roster, it's hard to believe the game once shunned a man for the color of his skin.

But Willie O'Ree discovered that the old-guard NHL had its unseen barriers.

Born in Fredericton, New Brunswick, in 1935, O'Ree had decent enough junior and minor league numbers in Eastern Canada to be considered for NHL employment. But he played a total of just 45 games, all with the Boston Bruins.

O'Ree, like Toronto's Herb Carnegie before him, found teams such as the Maple Leafs were not interested in his services because he was black.

Carnegie was called "the black Jean Beliveau" when he played in the minors, but had no calls from the NHL.

"There was no diversity in the league when I played," said O'Ree, who is now the director of Youth Development for NHL Diversity. "Though there is diversity now, there is room for expansion. It's a slow process, but we're moving in the right direction."

On January 18, 1958, the Bruins called him up for a game against the Canadiens. It had been more than a decade since Jackie Robinson had broke the color barrier in baseball.

"I know Robinson had it much tougher," O'Ree said of the Brooklyn Dodgers star, who sometimes had to stay at a different hotel than the white players.

> **"Racism isn't exclusive to hockey. Until we make things better in our everyday lives, we always will have problems."**
>
> – Willie O'Ree

When the curious questioned him about O'Ree, Bruins coach Milt Schmidt always said, "He isn't black, he's a Bruin."

After a two-game trial, O'Ree went back to play with Punch Imlach's Quebec Aces until the Bruins summoned him for a half-season in 1960–61. During that stint, he got into a vicious stick battle with Chicago Blackhawks' Eric Nesterenko, which saw both men tossed from the game. O'Ree heard some racial taunts and needed a police escort out of the rink. Detroit and New York fans could also be unkind.

"Part of the visitors' dressing room in the old Madison Square Garden had a wire window screen that bordered a public corridor," Scmidt said. "We opened it one night to let some fresh air in, but people started coming up and saying some very uncomplimentary things about Willie and poking their fingers through the screen. So one of our guys closed the window right on their fingers. That was the end of that."

O'Ree's best memory? Scoring the winning goal at home against Canadiens on January 1, 1961.

"I'll never forget the reception the Boston fans gave me after [a two-minute ovation]," O'Ree said later.

He was later traded to Montreal and completed his playing days as a minor-league star in Los Angeles and San Diego.

Despite the fact that O'Ree appeared in only 45 NHL games and scored only four goals, he had a professional career that lasted nearly 25 years.

The Backbone of the Russians

The first sight North Americans had of 20-year-old goaltender Vladislav Tretiak provoked more laughter than awe.

He was as thin as a rake, wore what looked like a modified baseball catcher's mask, and wore No. 20, a very unusual choice for a stopper. But more than 30 years later, Tretiak's influence on the position is still evident in the game.

Ed Belfour of the Maple Leafs, now third on the all-time list for NHL wins, was a devoted student and wears No. 20 in tribute. Jocelyn Thibault also credited Tretiak, and a host of young goalies came through his schools on both sides of the Atlantic.

Not bad for a kid who originally used his mother's field hockey stick to swat at rocks and only went between the pipes because it guaranteed him a coveted Red Army sports club uniform. Anatoli Tarasov, the Soviets' hockey guru, recognized Tretiak's potential and honed his skill and reflexes in several ingenious ways, on and off the ice.

When the 1972 Summit Series approached, Tretiak was ready, though Canadian scouts in Europe had the misfortune to see him only once, distracted in a bad outing that preceded his wedding day.

> **"The scouting reports said he couldn't stop a rolling basketball."**
> – John "Frosty" Forristall, Team Canada '72

When the series began at the Montreal Forum, Tretiak was beaten by two early goals, confused by the smaller Canadian rink, the noise and the music. But he foiled the best of the NHLers through the rest of the series, with the exception of Paul Henderson.

"I'll never forget it for the rest of my life," Tretiak said of Henderson's Game 8 goal. "It was a good goal, but I think maybe God gave him the chance to score on me. I told him, 'If I hadn't let that goal in, you wouldn't be famous.'"

Tretiak was toasted throughout the hockey world in the next few years as many of the Russian tactics and training methods were adopted. He yearned to play in the NHL, but there were gold medals to win for the rigidly controlled Soviet sports program. He had been retired for three years and was nearing 40 when the political barriers were finally dropped, allowing Eastern Europeans to play in the NHL.

"I was ready to come here for so long and I think I would have done well," said Tretiak, who is now in the Hall of Fame.

"I've dedicated my whole life to hockey and I would have given playing [in the NHL] 150%."

Tretiak's appearance at the Montreal Forum in 1972 began a love affair that would see him drafted by the team 11 years later. But the Russian Hockey Federation would have none of it, and playing for the Canadiens became an unrealized dream for Tretiak.

You Gotta Have Hart to Be a Hull

Fathers will pass the gift of hockey to their sons, but never had a son inherited the Hart Trophy until Brett Hull.

The torch was officially passed between the high-scoring wingers in 1991, when Brett beat out Wayne Gretzky for MVP, 25 years after his proud papa won the second of his two Harts. Brett's banner season featured 86 goals, a sum almost unimaginable in today's defense-minded NHL.

When Bobby Hull won his second Hart, he spent the $500 prize money on a blue-ribbon cow. Brett collected $100,000, enough to buy half a herd.

Bobby ended his career with 610 goals, achieving 50 goals five times for the Chicago Blackhawks. His decision to play for Winnipeg in the World Hockey Association in 1972 was a coup for the new league. He scored 300 more goals in the WHA, including 77 in 1974–75.

But Brett didn't stop scoring after 1991. He passed his father in career tallies and ended 2003–04 with 25 goals,

> **"Brett has never been in my shadow. I'd tell him something as a kid and he'd say, 'My coach tells me different.'"**
> – Bobby Hull on Brett Hull

> **"Maybe one day I will be equal to my Dad, but never better."**
> – Brett on Bobby

behind only Wayne Gretzky and Gordie Howe on the all-time list. His more than 100 playoff goals included the 1999 Cup winner for the Dallas Stars.

He was not as flamboyant a shooter as Bobby, whose lethal wind-up and slapshot struck fear in the hearts of lightly padded goalies in a time when many played without a mask. Brett would dart into position and snap a one-timer, always careful not to do any kind of celebratory schtick that would rile opponents. He made it look so easy that some critics early in his career labeled him as lazy.

"I don't see a lot of shadows," Brett once said, "because I don't have the puck very much."

But as he approaches age 40, he's became as important an elder statesman as his father. He's a player who doesn't hold back his feelings on the state of the game and has been voted the best interview by various media polls. He could wind up as a television analyst before long.

Bobby Hull was long considered one of the most prolific scorers in the history of the game. Amazingly, his son Brett may be even better.

Irvins Sr. and Jr. on Both Sides of the Leafs–Habs War

In 1999, when a TV technicians strike threatened to bar broadcasters from the opening game of Toronto's new Air Canada Centre, Dick Irvin was in a quandary.

The Hall of Fame broadcaster, son of the legendary coach of the same name, could not recall ever missing a Habs–Leafs game.

Born in 1932, five weeks before his dad coached the Leafs to their first Cup at the new Maple Leaf Gardens, Irvin Jr. first saw the teams clash in 1939–40. That was just before Dick Sr. changed cities and set the wheels in motion for three Montreal titles.

Father and son didn't see much of each other in the hockey season, as Dick Sr.'s work in the east saw him leave the family home in Saskatchewan and not return until the end of April. But during visits home, Dick Sr. would take his son to the radio station in Regina. Dick Jr. loved to watch the studio hum and became fascinated with the medium.

Dick Jr. moved to Montreal in 1951 to study accounting at McGill University, as the Leafs–Habs rivalry began its most colorful era. He had a great seat for the action when the team hired him, first as a statistician and then as an analyst.

"I think the best times were in the 1960s," Irvin Jr. said.

> **"If you looked at the high penalty-minute totals from those games, you saw fights, bench-clearing brawls – the works."**
>
> – Dick Irvin Jr.

"Punch Imlach was coaching for the Leafs against Toe Blake, just as the Leafs were coming around [to their four Cups that decade]. Imlach had a bit of showbiz about him and Blake didn't like it.

"It doesn't matter where either team is ranked when they play, because [either] building will be alive. Often, the fans put on a better show than the players."

The cold war used to extend to the broadcast booth. Irvin and the late play-by-play man, Danny Gallivan, would rarely mingle with their opposite numbers Bill Hewitt and Brian McFarlane. Gallivan was forbidden to use the seat in the Gardens' Gondola, from which Bill's father, Foster, had pioneered many aspects of hockey broadcasting.

"I'm always amazed by how many Leafs fans can be heard cheering when Toronto scores in Montreal," Irvin Jr. said. "You have to wonder how on earth they get those seats? It's the same when the Canadiens are in Toronto. [The rivalry] will never fade."

The only man besides Dick Sr. to coach both clubs is Pat Burns. He left the Habs hot seat in 1992, signing with the Leafs a couple of days later. In 2003, John Ferguson Jr., son of the great Habs enforcer, crossed family lines and became GM of the Leafs.

Dick Irvin Sr. was inducted into the Hockey Hall of Fame in 1958. Thirty years later, son Dick Jr. was granted the honor for his contributions as a broadcaster.

Wherever Henri Went, the Cup Was Sure to Follow

Henri Richard was a superb player, but a poor liar. Whenever he suggested that good fortune was the reason he won more Stanley Cups — 11 — than anyone else, people would politely remind him that 20 years, 1,046 career points, two years as league assists leader and a further 129 points in playoffs made him a bit more vital to the Canadiens' success than some fourth-line checker.

Despite the limitations of his five-foot-seven frame, Richard was better than any Canadiens prospect of his time. As a rookie in 1955–56, he had 40 points and two goals in the Cup final against Detroit, the first of five consecutive titles for the Habs.

The team's run continued into the spring of 1960, when Richard led the playoffs with 12 points, the year that big brother Maurice "Rocket" Richard completed his career with eight Cups.

Much smaller than Maurice, the Pocket Rocket celebrated 10 years in the NHL in 1966 with another Habs

> **"Had I been in any other city, New York or Chicago, I wouldn't have won as many Stanley Cups."**
>
> – Henri Richard

championship, scoring the 3–2 overtime winner against Detroit to clinch the Cup. The expanded NHL did not slow him down, and he closed the 1960s with two more titles.

In 1971, he joined an exclusive club of two-time Cup winning-goal scorers by eliminating the Chicago Blackhawks. He picked up 49 regular-season points that year and 12 in the playoffs.

The silver-haired Richard was also in on Montreal's 1973 championship, ushering in a new dynasty under coach Scotty Bowman. The 11th Cup made him the most prodigious player associated with the trophy among the 1,047 members of winning teams prior to 2004. Fellow Canadiens Jean Believeau and Yvan Cournoyer have won the Cup 10 times each.

It wasn't until after 1974–75, a playoff year in which Richard contributed three more points, that the Pocket Rocket retired.

Henri Richard's accomplishments on the ice earned him a spot in the Hockey Hall of Fame in 1979 and the Canadian Sports Hall of Fame in 1991.

Hockey Took a Liking to this Swedish Viking

North America's perception of Swedes up to the early 1970s didn't go much beyond blond, peace-loving designers of mod furniture.

In the hockey rink, they were considered to have limited skill and fortitude. "Chicken Swedes" was a popular term.

Oh, how wrong we were.

The lanky grandson of a reindeer herder from near the Arctic Circle came to the Toronto Maple Leafs in 1973 and opened the door for scores of countrymen in the next 30 years. Borje Salming was the highest-scoring defenseman in Leafs history, but it was his trail-blazing that earned him the admiration of friend and foe alike.

He could communicate only in hand gestures when he and Inge Hammarstrom arrived in Toronto. In his first game, he was named third star, but had to be pushed out the gate and shown the tradition of acknowledging the crowd's cheers.

Breaking in to the NHL just as the Broad Street Bullies of Philadelphia and their ilk had been established, Salming found himself just trying to survive on many nights. Goons of the day such as Dave Schultz would slap him around regularly.

But Salming didn't run and became regarded as the second-best defenseman in the league, after Montreal's

> **"Every Swede who draws an NHL salary should send some of it to Borje Salming."**
>
> – Harry Neale

Larry Robinson, twice finishing second for the Norris Trophy.

He was durable, fearlessly blocking shots and once suffering a 200-stitch gash on his face when he was accidentally stepped on by a skate.

During the Canada Cup in 1976, the Gardens fans gave Salming a long ovation after a win over a chippy American team. Future Leafs captain Mats Sundin, then a five-year-old in Stockholm, recalls his father calling him to the TV to show him a countryman getting such a reception in a foreign land, a memory that left a great impression.

Salming was once offered the captaincy of the Leafs, but declined, one of his greatest regrets. After playing through the worst of the Harold Ballard era in Toronto, Salming ended his career in 1989 as a Detroit Red Wing. He later played in his native country until the age of 40.

How much has the hockey world's view of Swedes changed? The Flyers, now run by one of Salming's greatest antagonists, Bobby Clarke, have a skilled Swedish defensemen in Kim Johnsson and a team loaded with Europeans. And goaltender Mikael Tellqvist, who wasn't even born when Salming began playing for Toronto, has incorporated artwork of Salming on his mask.

Mats Sundin says of Salming, "Every Swede respects Borje and pays him tribute for what he's done. For us – Swedish hockey players – he is the man who showed us the right way. He is a trailblazer."

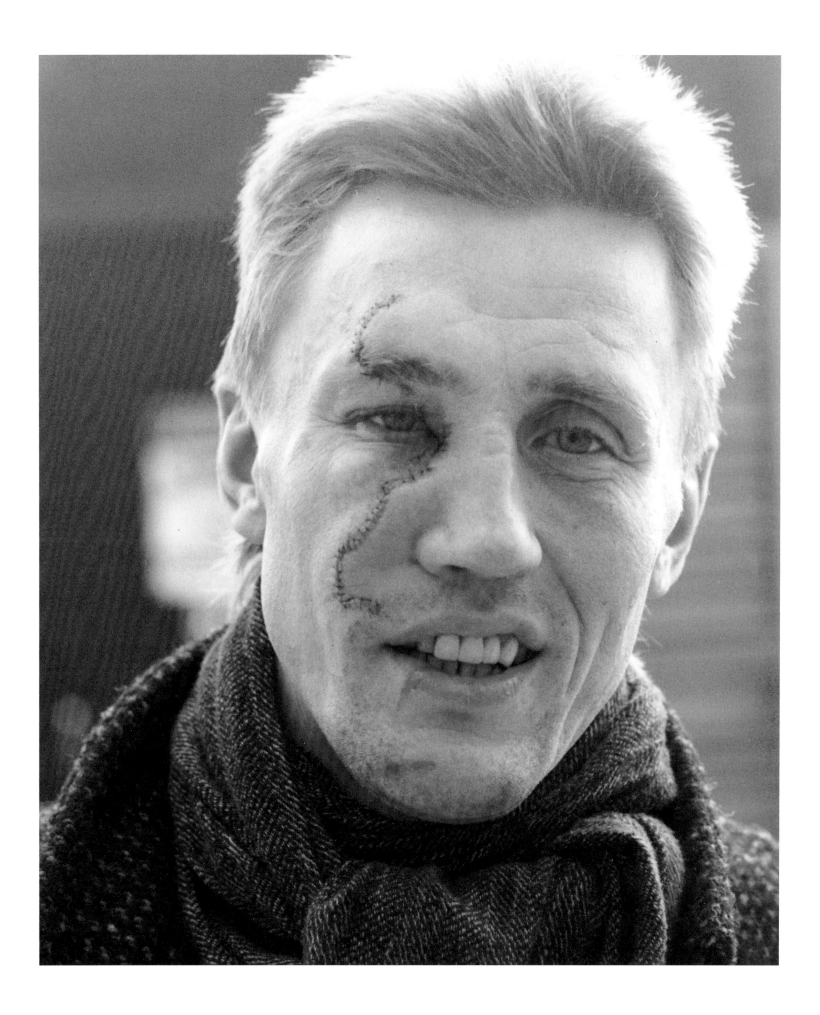

Brian Kilrea's 1,000 Ways to Win Friends and Influence People

Only Scotty Bowman has more coaching victories than Brian "Killer" Kilrea, who joined the 1,000 club on March 9, 2003, with a 4–2 home win over the Sudbury Wolves.

As with every other milestone in Killer's career, the phone started ringing as soon as he got in the door. Calls poured in from an alumni army of former Ottawa 67s, minor-league chums, the friends he made in the NHL with the New York Islanders and those he just met on the street.

"Brian Kilrea doesn't produce players, he produces people," the *Toronto Sun*'s Steve Simmons wrote.

He certainly produced champions, with three Ontario Hockey League titles in 1977, 1984 and 2001, and two Memorial Cups in 1984 and 1999. He's a four-time OHL coach of the year. Add to that his 15 seasons of playing in the minors, with 916 regular-season and 32 playoff games, and his 26 games played in the NHL, and he's been either on the bench or behind it for more than 3,000 games.

"And the best part is, I get paid for it," he told the *Sun*'s Ken Fidlin in 2003. "When I look back at all the experiences, I wouldn't trade them for anything. The people, the places, the years with Eddie Shore. I don't feel cheated at all. I feel lucky."

As the 10,328 fans at the Civic Centre saluted the final seconds of the win over Sudbury with a standing ovation, Kilrea began to get misty-eyed. He'd coached the 67s every year since 1974 — with the exception of two seasons (1984–85 and 1985–86) he spent as an assistant coach with the Isles.

Brian Bickell, Matt Foy, Matthew Albiani and Lou Dickenson scored to put Kilrea in the record book. Later that autumn, he went into the Hockey Hall of Fame in the builders' wing.

"The players have agents representing them now, so you don't get the personal touch of talking to them or their parents," Kilrea lamented. "But they remember when they get to the NHL not to burn any bridges or forget the things that got you there. The first thing I learned playing for Eddie Shore was humility. I'm proud that our guys have never forgotten us. When they come to town to play the Senators, they always stop by the night before and meet the new players."

"Between the ages of 16 and 20, you can go either direction, and he kept me in line," said Maple Leafs forward Gary Roberts. "He is one of the biggest reasons I am where I am today."

Kilrea is scheduled to be back behind the Ottawa bench in 2004–05, when he celebrates his 70th birthday.

> "He is a great coach, but he's a greater man. He's been a second father to a lot of us."
> — Ottawa 67 Adam Smyth on Brian Kilrea's 1,000th coaching victory

Kilrea played for 15 years in the minors before becoming a coach. In his time with the 67s, he has coached dozen of future NHLers.

Doug Jarvis Gets a Gold Star for Attendance

On October 8, 1975, Doug Jarvis glided into the face-off circle between Bob Gainey and Jim Roberts and won his first draw in the NHL.

He didn't take a night off for the next 12 years, compiling a record 964-game streak with three teams, a mark that is still years away from being broken.

"You could say the record snuck up on me," Jarvis said on December 26, 1986, in Hartford, the night he passed Gary Unger to become the NHL's Ironman with 915 games. "You'd pass someone on the ladder, and the next guy would be 200 games ahead, then you'd put it out of your mind."

Jarvis took good care of himself, crediting his Christian beliefs as the basis of his longevity. The streak was almost derailed in Game No. 761 in Detroit. A Randy Ladouceur hit caused a concussion, and Jarvis stayed overnight in the hospital. But he rejoined his Washington Capitals in St. Louis the next day. Today's concussion-sensitive regulations in the NHL likely would not have let him continue.

"He's got the most boring hockey card ever," former Whalers teammate Ray Ferraro said of the unbroken vertical line of 80 games played through the 1970s and 1980s.

His mother recalled that he had a near-perfect attendance record at school in Brantford, Ontario, refusing to make a fuss over a bruised leg that turned out to be broken.

Jarvis was drafted by the Maple Leafs, who erred in trading Jarvis for the long-forgotten Greg Hubick. Schooled in defensive tactics by Roger Neilson with the Peterborough Petes, Jarvis impressed Montreal coach Scotty Bowman from his first training camp, particularly on the draw.

Jarvis was part of the four Montreal Cups between 1976 and 1979.

"It's incredible what he's done," former teammate Bob Gainey said. "I played in 50 to 60 percent of the games in his streak and I know what he went through some nights."

One night, the Habs beat up on the Colorado Rockies, and Jarvis had a hat trick.

"As we were a checking line, he was almost embarrassed," Gainey said. "But inside every defensive player, there's an offensive player waiting to get out."

Unger's streak ended in discord in 1979 after Atlanta Flames coach Al MacNeil refused to let the aging, injured forward off the bench. Jarvis had a mutual agreement with the Hartford coaches to pack it in, voluntarily sitting out at the start of the 1987–88 season.

> **"I feel fortunate. There are so many things that can happen to you in games or practices."**
>
> – Doug Jarvis

Jarvis managed to score just 139 goals during his 964-game career. His best season was as a member of the 1981–82 Canadiens, when he scored 20 goals and added 28 assists.

Roger Had the Book on Rivals

The straight-laced guardians of hockey rules realized long ago that they couldn't outfox Roger Neilson.

So when he passed away in 2003, who better for the NHL to honor on the cover of the 2003–04 rules and regulation book than the coach who caused so many revisions to be printed?

As a junior coach, Neilson put Peterborough Petes defenseman Ron Stackhouse in goal for penalty shots and had him charge out to the shooter. If Neilson's team was killing a five-on-three power play, he kept sending players over the boards, since no amount of penalties could reduce his team to fewer than three skaters. When he pulled the goalie, he instructed him to drop his stick across the goal line to prevent empty-netters.

Each was a loophole he'd discovered in the rule book on long bus rides. Each was eventually closed.

"I lived with him a few years and there were about 1,000 other things he didn't try," said Jim Gregory, chairman of the Hockey Hall of Fame selection committee and Neilson's first NHL general manager with the Maple Leafs.

Neilson was also an astute playground baseball manager, deploying everything from the suicide squeeze to the hidden apple trick. The latter saw his catcher hide a peeled apple and throw it over to third base. The runner would trot home, only to be tagged out by the catcher with the real ball.

Neilson would coach 1,000 NHL games. He had some success, such as four winning records with the Leafs, Buffalo Sabres, New York Rangers and Philadelphia Flyers, the launch of the Florida Panthers and a 1982 Stanley Cup final appearance with the Vancouver Canucks.

There was plenty of hilarity along the way, too, as the personable, eccentric Neilson bumped heads with dinosaurs such as Leafs owner Harold Ballard. In Toronto, Neilson became the first NHL coach to use video as a tool, though he'd been experimenting with it since his Peterborough days, when he'd get high-school students to sneak camera equipment out of class to the rink.

"He made the development of hockey far more sophisticated than just having somebody's dad coaching the team," said Dick Todd, a Neilson protege, who later coached the Petes and was an assistant with the Rangers. "He's given people opportunities and opened doors for a lot of others," said Todd.

More than 1,400 people attended Neilson's funeral after his courageous battle with cancer finally ended.

> **"Coaches should read the rule book once a month. It's embarrassing in games if you don't know what's coming up."**
> – Roger Neilson

Roger Neilson's strength, courage and commitment to the game was recognized by the hockey world in 2002, when he was inducted into the Hall of Fame.

Badger Bob Made Believers of the Red, White and Blue

Badger Bob Johnson had religion, the kind that brought people to the rink. His calling was to get Americans to look past baseball, football and basketball and embrace the game of hockey.

"He thought about nothing else," a writer friend of his once said. "You'd be at a restaurant with him, the most stunning woman would walk by and have heads turning all over the place. But Bob would go on about a fourth-line checker on his team without taking his eyes off of you."

As much as he wanted hockey to grow in popularity in the United States, he was head coach for five years of the Calgary Flames, a hockey-mad Canadian city that suited him perfectly. As coach, he was obsessed with team meetings and preparation.

"I wore out two pairs of pads just sitting through the meetings," goaltender Don Edwards once joked.

Badger (the nickname came from his years coaching the University of Wisconsin) took the momentum from the post–Miracle on Ice years and helped develop many players south of the border. He died of brain cancer a few years before Team USA beat Canada for the 1996 World Cup and the NHL expanded into nine new American markets, events that surely would have made him happy.

Where Canada's national game stagnated to a degree in the early 1990s, Johnson-era players continued having an impact on the game right into the new century.

"There's no doubt he was a big inspiration on my career," said defenseman Gary Suter, who played for him with the Flames. "[When I was] a kid growing up in Madison, he was a big-time college coach. I went to all his hockey schools as a kid.

"I think he's a big reason I got drafted by the Flames. He was willing to take a chance on me. In my rookie year, he gave me a lot of ice time and confidence."

Johnson won Stanley Cups in 1990–91 and 1991–92 with the Pittsburgh Penguins, a team dominated by Mario Lemieux and Jaromir Jagr, but one infused with Johnson's personality.

"Bob Johnson is my No. 1 coach," said Jagr, who has had run-ins with his handlers through his career. "He will be forever. He was more fun."

After Johnson died, the Pens painted his motto "It's a great day for hockey" and his name on the ice. "He was so upbeat, so positive, he created such a very family-like atmosphere," Pens general manager Craig Patrick said.

"It's a great day for hockey."
– Bob Johnson

Badger Bob guided the University of Wisconsin to NCAA Championships in 1973, 1977 and 1981.

Fred Shero: The Fog Rolls Out

The Fog still has eager disciples long after his death. Fred Shero's legacy is still evident in the NHL and in Europe, despite the tendency to link him solely with the Broad Street Bullies' tactics of the mid-1970s.

The Winnipeg-born Shero was much more than the Philadelphia Flyers' dog handler. He inspired coaches such as Pat Quinn, Terry Crisp, Bill Barber and Alpo Suhonen, the last one of only two Europeans to coach an NHL team. Shero was just coming to prominence with the Cup-bound Flyers when a vacationing Suhonen asked for an audience, hoping to get a few pointers for his Finnish club team.

"When he drew something on the board, it was like watching an artist paint," Suhonen recalled. "He was a mysterious man but very friendly. He explained everything to me — systems, playbooks, text."

Shero, in turn, credited Soviet hockey guru Anatoli Tarasov's written strategies — "my bible," he called it. That shocked Suhonen, who wondered how a coach who embraced Tarasov's work could endorse the scorched-earth policy of the Flyers.

"He said you have to have a balance," Suhonen recalled. "He asked me to picture a pond with a duck on one side and a pier on the other. The duck keeps getting closer to the pier, even though it looks like it's not moving. His point was that the duck looks [calm] on top, but its legs are doing all the hard work that nobody sees."

Trying to create new practice drills and elaborate game plans, Shero would often lose himself in thought, hence his nickname.

> **"Go everywhere after the puck. Never back up if you can help it. Arrive first, and in ill humor."**
>
> —Fred Shero

"Athletes don't like to think," he once said. "You use distractions and surprise to hold their interest."

He convinced the entire Flyers team to live in Philly year-round so they could work out together. "Win today and we walk together forever," he urged his team as they went out to clinch the 1974 Cup against Boston.

The next season, sensing overconfidence setting in at team meetings, he would write messages on the ceiling, where he knew daydreamers would eventually be staring. But Shero's success didn't stop in Philly. In 1979, he coached the New York Rangers to the Cup final, within three wins of knocking off the mighty Canadiens of the day.

His innovations included the creation of the assistant coach position, once considered frivolous, but now a standard bench arrangement with two or more on the staff of all teams.

Shero died of cancer on November 24, 1990.

Shero played 15 years of pro hockey before moving behind the bench. A stay-at-home defenseman, he played 145 NHL games – all with the New York Rangers.

The Perfect Player:
In Praise of Bob Gainey

They should have recast the Frank Selke Trophy in the name of Bob Gainey. More than 25 years after its creation, no player has embodied its spirit as much as the man who won it the first four times as the NHL's best defensive forward.

Soviet hockey guru Anatoli Tarasov paid Gainey the ultimate compliment, calling him "the world's best technical player."

Raised in the Peterborough Petes system, and the eighth pick overall in 1973 by Montreal, Gainey was perfectly suited for coach Scotty Bowman's purposes.

Fittingly, Gainey went into the Hall of Fame in 1992 with Lanny McDonald, a high-scoring winger with the Maple Leafs and Calgary Flames, who was chosen four places ahead of Gainey in 1973. McDonald's Leafs were stymied twice in the playoffs in 1978 and 1979 by Gainey and the Canadiens.

> "If your bottom line is winning, you need those [defensive players]."
>
> – Bob Gainey

In the 1979 playoffs, Gainey won the Conn Smythe Trophy as Montreal won its fourth straight Stanley Cup. McDonald went on to Calgary and clashed with Gainey again in 1986 and 1989, when McDonald finally got his chance to carry the Cup before retiring.

"There was a game within a game when I lined up against Bob," said McDonald, a one-time Canada Cup teammate of Gainey's. "He was much more than a good defensive player, he was the most complete player I ever faced."

Gainey, who went on to a coaching career in France, as well as coaching and managing the Minnesota North Stars, Dallas Stars and most recently the Canadiens, was pleased to be among the first two-way players to receive Hall recognition.

Gainey had 239 goals and 262 assists in 1,160 games for Montreal, serving as team captain before his retirement in 1989.

Gainey returned to the Canadiens as general manager prior to the 2003–04 season in the hopes of restoring the franchise to greatness.

The Great Escape:
The Stastnys Jump to the NHL

Few people have pursued the NHL dream to the extent of the Stastny brothers, who put their well-being and that of their families in jeopardy.

Those thoughts raced through the minds of Peter and Anton Stastny in 1980 as they slipped away from the Czechoslovakian national team in the middle of the night and made a dash to Vienna, Austria, in a car with Quebec Nordiques owner Marcel Aubut and general manager Gilles Leger.

A third man — known to this day only as 007 — spirited Peter's pregnant wife Darina to meet them. Older brother Marian, who was married with three children, promised to come at a later date. Spotted in Vienna by the secret police, the younger Stastnys and their Canadian handlers made a harrowing getaway to the airport.

"Looking back, I wonder how we did it," Peter Stastny said. "We lived in a vicious, vicious system where the authorities would take revenge to make sure no one would follow."

Peter was sentenced to 18 months in jail in absentia for defecting. Marian was put under 24-hour surveillance and lost all his friends, who grew weary of being interrogated after each visit with him.

But after a year's planning by the Nordiques, Marian and his brood also escaped to Austria. He joined Peter and Anton, who had begun rewarding careers in the NHL. The brothers demonstrated the same scoring exploits they had shown at the Olympics and world championships. Peter's passes could find either opportunistic sibling on the wing.

"In Quebec, we were in paradise," Peter said. "Everybody loved to play in Quebec because of the atmosphere. When there were 17,000 people in the arena, you could feel the pride and excitement that this was their team. We felt their support every minute of every day."

The Nordiques, who were not long removed from the defunct WHA, became instant contenders and built a healthy rivalry with the Montreal Canadiens.

"It was unbelievably great for the sport," Peter said. "One year, we played three exhibition games against Montreal, eight regular-season games and seven playoff games. I thought Guy Carbonneau was attached to me. It was so much within the society of the people of Quebec, so much of their lives."

Peter played 15 NHL seasons, finishing his career in New Jersey and St. Louis, and made the Hall of Fame with 1,239 points. Anton lasted nine years and had 636 points in 650 games. Marian had 89 points as a 28-year-old rookie and played five NHL years, bowing out as a Maple Leaf.

> ## "We risked everything, even our lives."
> – Quebec Nordiques owner Marcel Aubut

When Marian finally joined his brothers in Quebec for the 1981–82 season, the trio combined for 107 goals and 300 points.

Manon Rheaume:
You Go, Goalie Girl!

In just one period of hockey, Manon Rheaume ended decades of women being shut out of pro sports. The Tampa Bay Lightning gave her the chance she'd wanted on September 23, 1992, when she played 20 minutes against the St. Louis Blues. The Quebec City native gave up two goals on nine shots at Tampa's Expo Hall.

"To face 100-mile-an-hour shots and the pressure, you don't do that to be the first woman," Rheaume said.

The crowd of 8,223 gave the five-foot-six Rheaume a standing ovation, and the old guard hockey men on hand were suitably impressed.

"She is legitimate," Blues president Ron Caron said. "She wasn't in there for her looks. She was there to stop pucks."

She stopped the first three shots, then gave up a long-range goal to Jeff Brown. She regained her composure and gave up just one more to Brendan Shanahan. Her best saves included a pad stop on Nelson Emerson. Wendell Young, the next Lightning goalie that night, also gave up two goals in one period.

"I gave her a seven-and-a-half out of ten," said

> **"I didn't do this just to have all the publicity. I did it because I love hockey."**
>
> – Manon Rheaume

Lightning president Phil Esposito, who admitted he was thinking more of the media attention for his new team when he first invited Rheaume to camp. "I remember my first NHL pre-season game, I was scared to death. There was a lot of pressure on her, but she handled it very well."

Rheaume wanted to get into an NHL regular-season game, but she settled for a three-year deal with Tampa's farm team at the time, the Atlanta Knights. She wrote a book, married Canadian roller hockey star Gerry St. Cyr, became a mother and an advocate for nutrition and continued her career with the Canadian national women's team.

She was also one of the biggest boosters to brother Pascal's career with the Atlanta Thrashers. They were briefly teammates with the Trois Rivières Draveurs of the Quebec Major Junior Hockey League, when Manon got to play a period in relief of Jocelyn Thibault.

"I'll always be known as Manon's brother," Pascal said of his famous sister. "But that's okay. She deserves the attention. "I'm really proud of all that she's accomplished."

In 1993–94 Manon posted a 5–0–1 record with the Knoxville Cherokees and the Nashville Knights of the East Coast Hockey League.

The All-Star Game's Skills Contests

Al Iafrate was given about five seconds of fame at each NHL All-Star game, and he made the most of it.

Year after year, the self-proclaimed Human Highlight Film and/or Wild Thing would blast his way into history by winning the hardest-shot event at the skills competition. Publications such as the *Guinness Book of Sports Records* would dutifully record each time Al Iafrate improved his velocity.

At the 1993 contest at the Montreal Forum, Iafrate was clocked at 105.2 miles per hour by the radar gun, his best ever.

"I don't practice it any more than any other young kid growing up," said the gentle giant from the Detroit suburbs, who was with the Washington Capitals when he set the mark. He retired after long bouts with knee problems in 1997–98.

He's the only man to get over 100 m.p.h. three times, though Al MacInnis reached that twice in winning the event six times overall. An eye injury prevented MacInnis from defending his title in 2004 in St. Paul, Minnesota, where Sheldon Souray of the Montreal Canadiens and Adrian Aucoin of the New York Islanders tied at 102.2.

"Iafrate must have had a rocket launcher," said Souray, who felt he couldn't have connected on his shot any better.

"It's a gift from God."

– Al Iafrate

The record for fastest skater is held by Mike Gartner, a spry 36-year-old when he did 13.386 seconds in one lap of Boston's Fleet Center in 1996. He also ranks second at 13.510, set three years earlier.

"Age doesn't matter," Gartner said. "Some days you're 25 and feeling 45 and sometimes the opposite. There's not a trick to it, though most races of any kind are won on the first turn."

When it comes to target shooting, few have the shooting eye for four styrofoam bulls' eyes that former Bruin Ray Bourque possessed. He owned the event, winning or tying eight times, including two consecutive 4-for-4 years.

"One or two times is lucky, but eight is no coincidence," goaltender Sean Burke said, after Bourque won his last title as a Colorado Avalanche in front of the Pepsi Center home crowd in 2001. "That's incredible to watch."

Bourque's secret?

"Maybe to stay relaxed and make sure the puck is flat when it's passed to you," he said.

In 2004, Jeremy Roenick of the Philadelphia Flyers became just the third man to go 4-for-4, joining Bourque and Mark Messier, who had done it once.

| Prior to his career-ending eye injury, MacInnis's slapshot was feared by every shot-blocking defenseman in the NHL.

Foster Hewitt:
Voice of the Maple Leafs

For decades, no one saw Foster Hewitt's face, yet his voice brought a hockey game to life. He never picked up a shovel or a hammer, but many credit him with building Maple Leaf Gardens.

He didn't serve in World War II, but he was the man every soldier, sailor and airman could turn to when they felt the pangs of separation from home. Few of those listeners cared that the games he called were two weeks old.

Observing radio silence, airmen on missions weren't supposed to tune in to his broadcasts. But that didn't stop the Canadian crew of a Lancaster bomber during one sortie. The pilot called a mock Toronto game over the intercom à la Hewitt, with a winning goal so descriptive that the Leaf-hating tail-gunner argued it was offside.

"No single individual has contributed more to the success of hockey as we know it today than Foster Hewitt," said NHL president Clarence Campbell in the mid-1970s.

Hewitt pioneered hockey on radio on March 22, 1923, when the *Toronto Star*, owner of station CFCA, sent the cityside reporter to cover a seniors game between Parkdale and a visiting team from Kitchener at Mutual St. Arena. Hewitt initially balked at covering a sports event, but the seeds of a career change were planted that night.

Soon he was the voice of the newly christened Leafs, and his famous call, "He shoots, he scores," was heard coast to coast.

> **"Hello, Canada and hockey fans in the United States and Newfoundland . . . and a special hello to our Canadian forces around the world."**
>
> – Foster Hewitt

When Leafs boss Conn Smythe wanted to get investors for a new arena in 1930, almost 100,000 people answered Hewitt's message to write in for a program, carefully tucking the requested dime inside the envelope. That convinced Smythe and some nervous investors to go ahead with the project that became the Gardens.

As it neared completion, Smythe realized Hewitt's importance and asked where he wanted his broadcast location to be. Hewitt walked up and down the stairs at an Eaton's department store, watching the faces on the main-floor crowd, until he settled on the fifth floor as a comfortable perch.

The booth, later immortalized as the Gondola for its resemblance of an air ship's gondola, was hung at 54 feet up from center ice.

Hewitt's second home was accessible only by a narrow catwalk that kept most frightened visitors and dignitaries away. But his tenure covered the greatest days of Leafs hockey, and he made the team the best-known in the land. He inspired such loyalty in the Leafs fans of his time, that even today their children and grandchildren often cheer for the Leafs over their hometown teams.

Hewitt brought his son Bill into the business when televised hockey arrived in the 1950s, but still had the stamina to handle the Canada–Russia series in 1972.

He retired a few years later.

> Foster Hewitt called the first game televised by the CBC on October 11, 1952. It was a match-up between the Montreal Canadiens and the Toronto Maple Leafs.

The Cannonading Career of Danny Gallivan

A large graduating class of play-by-play men has emerged since the National Hockey League expanded to 30 teams.

But though he inspired many of them, Danny Gallivan can never himself be duplicated. And no one knows that more than the people in his own business.

"The lasting memory is of the Montreal Canadiens carrying the Cup off the ice with Danny's voice the last you heard," long-time broadcast partner Dick Irvin Jr. said. "Wherever he went, to banquets or speaking engagements, Danny was the star."

Gallivan, a native of Sydney, Nova Scotia, got his break in radio in the late 1940s, when he called an amateur game in Montreal back to a station in Halifax. He came to the attention of Canadians in 1952, the year of the first *Hockey Night in Canada* telecast.

"My father was coaching the team then, and he took Danny into the dressing room before [the first game]," Irvin Jr. said. "Dad told him, 'Take a good look at these players, because you won't be able to keep up with them when the game starts.'"

But Gallivan did keep pace with the firewagon Habs as they won six Stanley Cups in his first eight years and 15 overall before he retired in 1984 because of vision

> "I think Danny once got a letter from an English teacher: 'Dear Mr. Gallivan, there is no such word as cannonading.' To which Danny wrote back: 'There is now.'"
>
> – Dick Irvin

problems. With no one having held the TV job before Gallivan arrived, he was free to pepper his dialogue with his personal descriptive phrases.

The holder of a Bachelor of Arts degree from St. Francis Xavier University, he endeared himself to his audience with such classics as "cannonading shot," "scintillating save" and "Savardian Spinnerama." And let's not forget the ever-popular "big Robinson ad-libbing his way to center. . ."

He was conscripted for games involving a woeful Toronto team in the early 1980s. Shocked by the state of the team's effort one night, he remarked "the Leafs are playing as ragged as a hobo's jacket."

Gallivan, who resisted the technological advances in his medium, clutched a microphone years after lapel mikes were invented. Sometimes he had to almost shout to be heard above the din at the Forum that followed a Canadiens goal.

"I am perhaps more fortunate than most broadcasters, in that I work in front of 18,000 to 19,000 voluble and knowledgeable fans," Gallivan once said.

"There is no way I could get excited about broadcasting in Oakland in front of 2,500 or 3,000 fans."

Gallivan, Foster Hewitt, Dick Irvin and Bob Cole have all been enshrined in the Hockey Hall of Fame for their work on *Hockey Night in Canada*.

The Zebras Who Keep Control of the NHL Jungle

Imagine if referees and linesmen had to be recruited through the newspapers. Here's how the ad might read:

"WANTED: A few good men to travel a 30-city circuit on short notice for up to nine months. Must be in good physical condition, be patient with all manner of travel snags and still be punctual for work.

"Must be able to endure verbal abuse in the workplace and physical abuse such as high sticks, punches and kicks, as well as hard rubber disks fired at high speeds at lightly protected areas of the body. Ability to dodge beer cans, programs, rubber chickens, batteries and coins is appreciated.

"Might also be required to retrieve balloons and beach balls, clean up hats after hat tricks, and corral the odd cat, mouse, squirrel or dead octopus. Ability to make correct decisions in a split second a must. Apply to the National Hockey League."

Linesman Ray Scapinello liked the life so much he stayed on the job for 33 years, retiring at the end of the 2003–04 playoffs. When he started on October 17, 1971, the opposing goaltenders were Gump Worsley of the Minnesota North Stars and Roger Crozier of the Buffalo Sabres. Both are in the Hockey Hall of Fame, and the 57-year-old Scapinello is likely headed there too.

"Conditioning has got to be one of the biggest differences I've seen since I began," the native of Guelph said. "I can remember swinging a rusty pair of skates over my shoulder and just showing up for camp."

By the time Scapinello retired, the officials as well as the players had made many advances in conditioning, from personal trainers to state-of-the-art video. Some officials didn't like the gradual introduction of an eye in the sky to challenge their authority, or the arrival of the two-referee system a few years ago, but the faster speed of the game meant adapting.

It still comes down to the officials being tough but fair and being accorded respect from the players and coaches.

"We know the players have high emotions, but it would be pretty sad if we went nuts, too," Scapinello said. "We usually have a great rapport with the players. [Leafs penalty-minute leader Tie] Domi can say some really witty things after a fight."

Scapinello worked 2,500 games; referee Terry Gregson ended his 25-year career at the same time.

> **"I tell the young officials to write down everything weird that happens to them. It'll make a helluva book one day."**
> – Ray Scapinello

Often the best skater on the ice, Scapinello, now retired, is headed for the Hockey Hall of Fame.

Singing the Praises of Hockey

The emotion generated on the ice, coupled with hockey's checkered characters, has provided inspiration for wonderful stories now spanning three centuries.

Very few have been set to music, yet most of the ones that have are now classics, if only in the camp sense.

Think of Stompin' Tom Connors's "The Hockey Song," written by the Maritime troubadour in 1972. It's now an arena staple: *Hello out there/we're on the air. . .*

"I truly did want it to become the anthem that it has," Connors said. "I tried to write it in a way where I was in an arena and hearing it myself. It's a song that took its life from kids who heard it in arenas. A lot of NHL players have told me that they grew up with it."

"The Hockey Song" didn't get much airplay upon release, but Connor's travels helped it sustain a pulse, as did the odd radio program, including the weekly Dr. Demento novelty show, which brought it to the attention of a small American audience. The gradual rise of recorded music in arenas brought it back to life in 1992, when the Ottawa Senators and the Leafs began to play it.

The Leafs' Eddie Shack was already one of the league's wildest players when a Toronto singer cut "Clear the Track, Here Comes Shack" (*He knocks 'em down and he gives 'em a whack*). Leafs goaltender Johnny Bower sang "Honky the Christmas Goose," and defenseman Jim Schoenfeld of the Sabres cut an album in the 1970s.

> **"I was just a little forward and you were on defense."**
> – "Forgive My Misconduct,"
> Dione and the Puck Tones

With the Los Angeles Kings located in the heart of the entertainment industry, it was only a matter of time before there was a crossover. At the height of their scoring prowess in the mid-1980s, the "Triple Crown Line" of Marcel Dionne, Dave Taylor and Charlie Simmer cut "Forgive My Misconduct" as Dionne and the Puck Tones. Other 45s included "The Ballad of Team Canada ('72)" and "That Boston Dandy (Bobby Orr)."

A three-CD set of hockey arena music was released in Canada in the 1990s. Classics such as "Rock and Roll, Part 2" by Gary Glitter and Queen's "We Will Rock You" have become staples during timeouts.

"I'm delighted to see people in North America still getting pleasure out of it," Glitter told NBC in 1991. "Obviously, they have great taste in music. Tell everyone in North America to enjoy their sports and enjoy their rock and roll."

But the most recognized hockey tune is an instrumental. The *Hockey Night in Canada* theme was created in the 1960s by Delores Claman, who wrote for McLaren Advertising in Toronto. She was asked for some music to introduce the revamped TV show. Envisioning a clash of medieval knights, Claman came up with a stirring, brassy number that even now calls Canadians to their TV sets every Saturday.

I "The Hockey Song" has become an anthem for the game and turned Stompin' Tom Connors into a Canadian icon.

Flying to Glory on the Wings of KLM

If you played international hockey in the 1980s, there were two acronyms you feared. One was CCCP, identifying the Russian national team sweaters, the other was KLM, that team's most vaunted forward line. Vladimir Krutov, Igor Larionov and Sergei Makarov were united toward the end of the 1970s, with Krutov and Larionov graduating from the 1979 world juniors and joining the older Makarov.

Larionov was the only member of the trio not at the Lake Placid Olympics in 1980 for the American upset, but the group blasted all opposition from then on, en route to the gold in 1984. Together with defensemen Slava Fetisov and Alexei Kasatonov, they became known as the Russian Five or the Larionov Five.

KLM was the brainchild of Victor Tikhonov, the harddriving Red Army and national team coach, whose methods would later help drive the five to escape to the NHL. But at the time, choosing the nimble Larionov to run the show in the middle and letting the five develop as a unit was a radical move in hockey.

Larionov was the last piece of the puzzle. The others all played for the powerful Central Red Army, while Larionov was happy with the lesser-known Khimik club. Tikhonov

> **"On the day I put Larionov together with Makarov/Krutov, that somehow lightened my spirits."**
>
> – Viktor Tikhonov

essentially gave him no choice but to change teams, especially after the night Larionov had five assists against Red Army, four against a line with Krutov and Makarov on the wings.

Starting with victories in the 1981 world championships and the 1981 Canada Cup, KLM and the Soviets ruled the world scene until a lose at the '84 Canada Cup. They came back and won Olympic gold in 1988.

But later in the decade, the restricted lives the stars endured pushed them to seek new challenges in the NHL. With youngsters such as Alex Mogilny and Sergei Fedorov set to defect, authorities slowly relaxed and the Five were gradually allowed to leave.

"We've been loyal to Red Army for ten years or so, but today I no longer consider myself a serviceman," Larionov told a Moscow paper in announcing that he was quitting. He and Krutov went to the Vancouver Canucks, Makarov joined Sergei Priakin in Calgary, and Fetisov and Kasatonov were signed by New Jersey.

Makarov won the NHL's Calder Trophy in 1990, while Larionov continued playing into the 2003–04 season. He and Fetisov won Stanley Cups with Detroit and triumphantly took the Cup back to Russia.

Often referred to as the "Russian Gretzky," Larionov (right) began his NHL career at the age of 30 and played 15 seasons with Vancouver, San Jose, Detroit, Florida and New Jersey.

Playoff Hope Springs Eternal in the Great White North

"Two Canadian teams and that many people singing our anthem . . . it's hard for you to understand how great it is to come back to Canada and be in this environment." — Calgary Flames' coach Darryl Sutter during the series with Vancouver.

O Canada was heard a lot in the 2004 NHL playoffs, the biggest representation by Canadian teams since 1996. The Flames, Vancouver Canucks, Toronto Maple Leafs, Montreal Canadiens and Ottawa Senators all qualified, with the Edmonton Oilers in contention until the final weekend of the regular season.

"It's so great to see," said *Hockey Night in Canada*'s venerable play-by-play man Bob Cole. "It didn't look good for a couple of these teams a few years ago, but they've come back strong. And it's been great for our ratings."

Hockey Night in Canada pulled in their best viewer numbers in a decade as the Leafs/Senators and Flames/Canucks both went seven games in their respective opening round series. The Leafs and Senators were no strangers to playoff rivalry, as they met for the fourth time in five years. The Corel Centre was never louder as 18,500 fans of

> **"Two Canadian teams and that many people singing our anthem...it's hard for you to understand how great it is to come back to Canada and be in this environment."**
>
> – Calgary Flames' coach Darryl Sutter during the series with Vancouver

both teams jammed in. Ottawa sensed its time had come after years of last place finishes, patient drafting and play-off heartbreak. But the result was same old, same old, for the Sens, who forced a deciding game with an overtime win over Toronto on home ice, but couldn't follow it up in Game 7. The Leafs were subsequently bounced from the playoffs by the Philadelphia Flyers in the next round.

Martin Gelinas helped the Flames celebrate their first play-off appearance in seven years, by notching the Game 7 overtime goal after Vancouver had produced a last-minute regulation goal. Vancouver, minus rugged forward Todd Bertuzzi, was also affected by the loss of starting goaltender Dan Cloutier who suffered a right ankle injury in Game 3 of the series. Up next for Calgary was perennial powerhouse Detroit. The Flames won the spirited match-up 4–2 and then disposed of the San Jose Sharks in similar fashion. Captain Jarome Iginla, who suffered the most of any Flame as year after year passed without a post-season berth, delivered a memorable spring, leading Calgary to its first Stanley Cup final since 1989.

The Canadiens pulled a first-round upset after spotting the Boston Bruins a 2–0 and 3–1 series lead, then came back for their own seventh-game thriller. Their run ended against the eventual Stanley Cup Champs, the Tampa Bay Lightning in the next round. The Lightning went on to defeat the Flames in a heated seven-game final.

The Coach Who Can't Be Cornered

Who else but Don Cherry could be in hot water with the Canadian Broadcasting Corporation and at the same time score so high on the CBC's vote for Greatest Canadian?

Who else but Don Cherry could run afoul of federal language officials and yet be approached to run for political office?

Who else but Don Cherry could make ridiculous assertions about European players on *Hockey Night in Canada*, but have every kid in the nation take his word on the merits of shot-blocking, hitting clean and even fighting?

Who else but Don Cherry detests hot-dog players, but has the most outrageous wardrobe on the tube, simultaneously appearing on best- and worst-dressed lists?

In 2004, when the CBC slapped a seven-second delay on Coach's Corner following Cherry's rant that most players who wear visors in the NHL are "Europeans and French guys," the whole nation was caught up in the "censorship" debate.

"It seems every time there is anything bad in the world, it's me," Cherry told the *Toronto Sun*. "But I guess if you are going to give it out, you have to take it. They have been upset with me for 23 years, since the day I took over."

Cherry could never have made it on the pension he earned as NHL player. Despite a long and colorful minor-league career, the Kingston, Ontario, native appeared in exactly one game, during the 1955 playoffs for Boston.

He made his name as a coach, the perfect complement to the lunch-bucket Bruins of the mid 1970s. But after a falling-out with general manager Harry Sinden and a brief stint with the Colorado Rockies, he was looking for a new line of work.

He started popping up as guest analyst on regional games in the U.S., before HNIC producer Ralph Mellanby paired him with Ron MacLean on Coach's Corner. Cherry was unpolished and remains so, mispronouncing names, gabbing on about Bobby Orr, the Bruins, his dog, Blue, and even kissing players from Kingston. But he genuinely wants the game to thrive and is eager to show young viewers the do's and don'ts. And, of course, the beer, hall crowd loves him, from his high-collared shirts and themed ties to the poppy he wears with pride every Rememberance Day in Canada.

MacLean is the perfect sidekick; in fact, he used to boot Cherry under their seats near the end of Coach's Corner to signal in that their five minutes of fame was up for another week. MacLean can open the floodgates for a Cherry rant, be his foil on a hot topic, or channel the conversation elsewhere if need be.

"When I started in TV, I had no trade, no education. I was a construction worker," Cherry said. "So everything I have, I owe it to Ralph. He said 'Grapes, pronounce [names] any way you like, that's your charm.' The TV brass stormed in and told Ralph to get me off TV. He said, 'If he goes, I go.' I stayed."

> "I feel that some day, they're going to come to me and say, 'well, you've just gone too far.'"
>
> – Don Cherry

> Many would argue that Cherry's opinion may not be educated, but there is no doubt that it's informed. He spent 25 years in pro hockey as a player and a coach and won the Jack Adams Trophy as Coach of the Year in 1976.

Index

Photo Credits